Celebrating
Reconciliation
10 Penitential Services

Linda K. Valasik, H.M.

Linda Valasik, H.M., has served as a Director of Religious Education and a parish pastoral minister for the past 21 years in various dioceses throughout the United States. She has a B.S. Ed. from St. John College in Cleveland, an M.R. Ed. from Aquinas College in Grand Rapids and an M.A. in Ministry from Seattle University.

The Publishing Team
Rose Schaffer, H.M., M.A., President/Chief Executive Officer
Bernadette Vetter, H.M., M.A., Vice President
Donna Emerson, CSJ, M.A., Coordinator of Parish Publications
Mary Jane Simmons, H.M., M.A., Consultant

Cover and Illustrations
Krina K. Walsh, B.S.I.D.

Nihil Obstat   The Reverend David J. Walkowiak, J.C.D., MDiv
Censor Deputatis

Imprimatur   The Most Reverend Anthony M. Pilla, D.D., M.A.
Bishop of Cleveland

Given at Cleveland, Ohio on 18 December 1995.

The *nihil obstat* and *imprimatur* are official declarations that a book is free of doctrinal or moral error. No implication is contained therein that those who have granted the *nihil obstat* and *imprimatur* agree with the contents, opinions, or statements expressed.

Table of Contents

Introduction

God's Work of Reconciliation

So for anyone who is in Christ, there is a new creation: the old order is gone and a new being is there to see. It is all God's work; he reconciled us to himself through Christ and he gave us the ministry of reconciliation. I mean, God was in Christ reconciling the world to himself, not holding anyone's faults against them, but entrusting to us the message of reconciliation.

So we are ambassadors for Christ; it is as though God were urging you through us, and in the name of Christ we appeal to you to be reconciled to God. For our sake he made the sinless one a victim for sin, so that in him we might become the uprightness of God. [1]

Ministers who facilitate the process of reconciliation are facilitating the heart of the gospel. The gospel reveals to us Jesus's way of living, and the path of reconciliation with God, others, and self leads us to walk this way of life. Reconciliation is essential for a follower of Jesus.

But reconciliation is risky territory, and it is terribly hard work. This is so because reconciliation is about conversion. Reconciliation means naming and claiming our weaknesses and then choosing, with God's help, to be different.

Yet, reconciliation is not a private affair. It is relational. When we wish to be reconciled, we must gather with the community to enter this process. It is in the midst of the faith community that we find the power of God's reconciling Spirit.

Purpose

The purpose of this book is to provide penitential services which can be celebrated in a faith community. These services are meant to ultimately deepen peoples' understanding of and desire for the journey of conversion. While they do not include the Sacrament of Reconciliation, these services are intended to ready communities for an experience with a loving and life-giving God.

---

[1] 2 Cor 5:17–21, *New Jerusalem Bible* (New York: Doubleday, 1985), 1916.

Overview

An important development in Catholic spirituality resulting from the Second Vatican Council is a deeper awareness of the true nature of sin. Human imperfection, failures, and accidents do not generally come under the heading of serious sin—grave wrong done knowingly and purposefully. A community of faith, responding to this deepening awareness, will benefit from opportunities to reflect on root causes of sin in the human heart. This reflection can stimulate formation of conscience. The penitential services in this book provide that opportunity by offering not only Scripture and prayer, but also music, participation, Scripture reflection and environment options. Busy ministers, who wish to tailor the service to an individual faith community, will find the offerings in this book a strong support in facilitating spiritual growth.

The ten penitential services address distinct times in the liturgical year and the spiritual journey. Services 1 through 3 are for use in Advent, while 4 through 6 are for the time of Lent. They generally correspond to the A, B, C Scripture Cycles. The images and symbols of Advent and Lent are similar in the seasonal readings and so it is possible to use these services interchangeably among the cycles, if desired.

Services 7 through 10 were written for particular times of personal renewal or recommittment. They are shorter and simpler because they are intended for groups already in a process of prayer and reflection. Suggested times for their use are:

"Living in the Spirit" can be used during a retreat focusing on the Holy Spirit, or at the season of Pentecost, or while discerning leadership or ministries.

"Being Lost, Being Found" can be used during a women's day of prayer, a retreat weekend, or a parish day of celebration when parishioners gather for spiritual revitalization.

"Forgiving in Love" is for couples. The communal form of this service can be used with a group in a retreat experience, during an anniversary day of prayer or during a marriage or engaged encounter weekend. The private form of this service is intended to be used by an individual couple. It was written at the request of pastoral counselors and spiritual directors who recognized the need of couples for healing in their marriage. It can be easily used by all couples, even those in an interfaith marriage.

"Called to Reconciliation" is a service that speaks of servant leadership. All ministers who exercise leadership in their faith community—parish council persons, directors of ministries, service groups, social groups, staffs, and teams—may be able to pray with this penitential service.

Tailoring Penitential Services to Your Faith Community

Choosing Among Options

The uniqueness of each faith community is to be recognized. Its prayer and spirituality are shaped by its particular journey and gifts. When preparing one of these penitential services, the facilitating minister must choose music selections from the resources section following each service. Some services offer options for a sung or recited responsorial psalm. Choices are to be made here as well. You will also find Scripture reflection ideas and suggestions for environment. However, these are simply ideas. If they are not suited to your faith community, make your own choices that complement and enrich the community's prayer and help members enter into reconciliation. You, as minister in the community, know the needs of the community best.

Participation

Since reconciliation is God's work in the community, it is appropriate to have broad participation from those present, according to their ministries. It follows then that the leader of prayer may be either an ordained or a lay person. The Scripture message of penance and reconciliation is presented clearly through the faith and skill of a prepared reader. The prophetic meaning of God's word can be brought to life in the Scripture reflection of a man or woman who discovers that word in their daily circumstances. The communal prayer and the communal expression of sorrow tell of God's merciful and constant love in all gathered. Each person present plays a role in the service and can be invited into conscious and active participation.

Periods of Silence and Reflection

Periods of silence are often indicated in the services. These periods provide the necessary reflection time to be in touch with God and with ourselves. Interior silence is not a frequent experience for most people, but it is essential to hear God's voice. The person leading the service must know the assembly well enough to judge the length of this period of silence. It should "stretch" the individual's experience, but not tax it.

Examination of Conscience

> Sin is being today, just like we were yesterday.
> Sin is hearing the word and not responding to it.[2]

Jesus established a new way of life, a new covenant. This new covenant is expressed in the two great laws of love—love of God and love of neighbor. The Christian Scripture is replete with ways to fulfill this covenant. It is from here that we examine our conscience. The examination of conscience in all services flows from the Scripture readings. These questions facilitate reflection on our relationship with God, with others, and with self. The resources section following each service offers ways to present the examination of conscience to the faith community. It is very important to do this slowly and prayerfully, giving people time to consider each question.

---

[2] Thomas Richstatter, O.F.M., *The Reconciliation of Penitents* (Washington, D.C.: Federation of Diocesan Liturgical Commissions, 1987), 41.

A Hope

This book was originally written to fill a practical purpose, that of providing prepared, flexible penitential services of quality for those of you who are already busy with many pastoral responsibilities. Hopefully, it will also stimulate your reflection about God's gift of reconciliation and the prayer needs of your faith community. There is no greater healing than to be reconciled before God and among ourselves. May these pages assist you in bringing that joy to others.

How to Use This Resource

In preparing this service to be printed for the assembly, select and type in, prior to printing, your choices for the following parts.

Choose song from music suggestions in resources section following service.

Select response from music suggestions in resources section.

Make choice from alternatives given in music suggestions.

See suggestions given in resources section.

Waiting in Joyful Hope
Gathering Rites

Opening song

Greeting

> In the name of the Father, and of the Son, and . . .

> May the grace, mercy and peace of our loving God be with you.

All: And also with you.

Introduction

> Waiting is the work of Advent. But what is our waiting about? Jesus came long ago, and we believe that we have forgiveness for our sins.

> Our waiting has a distant focus and is one firmly marked with hope. We await the new heavens and the new earth, the time when the justice of God will reside in all people's hearts. Let us pray now with and for each other in this time of waiting.

Opening prayer

> Let us pray. *(Period of silence)*

> Patient God, you want all people to be saved, but that is as much our choice as yours.

> You ask us to stay awake to your coming but we do not easily recognize you because we are often distracted by our own concerns.

> Give us the grace to know that our days are the waiting time in which we welcome or reject your love.

> Help us to embrace our role of witnessing to your compassionate and saving presence among all people, now and in the time to come.

> We ask this through Jesus, our Lord and Redeemer.

All: Amen.

Celebration of the Word of God

First reading: *2 Pt 3:8–14*

Response *(followed by a brief period of silence)*

Gospel acclamation

Gospel: *Mk 13:33–37*

Scripture Reflection

At Advent Time

The Coming of God's Reign

Gathering

Opening song

Greeting

> Grace, mercy, and peace
> from God who is our hope,
> and from Jesus Christ who is our redemption.

Response: Amen.

Introduction

> Sisters and brothers, our God is a God who is always coming—long ago in Bethlehem, in the future at the end of the world, today in the exchanges we have with others.

> Because of our Baptism we have a large part to play in God's coming into our world each day. We gather now in this season of "coming" to reflect on the ways and reasons God's reign has been blocked in our lives and in the lives of those we touch.

Opening prayer

> Let us pray. *(period of silence)*

> God of compassion
> we come before you
> seeking forgiveness for our sins
> and the strength, modeled by your prophet John,
> to advance your reign in our world.

> Renew us with your healing love.

> Fill us with the desire
> to turn from prejudice and pride,
> materialism and selfishness.

> We ask this through Jesus your son and our brother.

Response: Amen.

Celebration of the Word of God

First reading: *Is 11:1–10*

  (followed by period of silence)

Responsorial psalm: *Ps 72:1–2, 5, 10–15, 17–19*

Group 1
  O God, with your judgment endow the king,
    and with your justice, the king's son;
  He shall govern your people with justice
    and your afflicted ones with judgment.
Group 2
  May he endure as long as the sun,
    and like the moon through all generations.
Group 1
  The kings of Tarshish and the Isles shall offer gifts;
    the kings of Arabia and Seba shall bring tribute.
  All kings shall pay him homage,
    all nations shall serve him.
Group 2
  For he shall rescue the poor man when he cries out,
    and the afflicted when he has no one to help him.
  He shall have pity for the lowly and the poor;
    the lives of the poor he shall save.
  From fraud and violence he shall redeem them,
    and precious shall their blood be in his sight.
Group 1
  May he live to be given the gold of Arabia,
    and to be prayed for continually;
    day by day shall they bless him.
Group 2
  May his name be blessed forever;
    as long as the sun his name shall remain.
  In him shall all the tribes of the earth be blessed;
    all the nations shall proclaim his happiness.
Group 1
  Blessed be the LORD, the God of Israel,
    who alone does wondrous deeds.
Group 2
  And blessed forever be his glorious name;
    may the whole earth be filled with his glory.

  All: **Amen. Amen.**

Gospel: *Mt 11:2–11*

Scripture reflection

Examination of conscience

- My Baptismal dignity gives me the power to announce, like John, Jesus presence in our world. What have I done to know and understand Jesus' message better?

- What reading or thinking, praying or discussing with others have I done to allow the Spirit of knowledge and understanding to strengthen me?

- What cripples me or causes me to stumble in my relationship with Jesus when I hear his teachings?

- What keeps me from praying more openly with God?

- What keeps me from praying more genuinely about the needs of all people in the world?

- How have my actions proclaimed the values of Jesus—in my home, my place of work, my neighborhood, my social contacts?

- How do I respond to others who seem to be blind or deaf to God's love?

- What attitude of mine keeps others from being influenced by God?

- In what circumstances do I find it hardest to model Jesus' way of thinking and living? Why?

- What are my attitudes toward the poor and afflicted, the outcast, the marginal people in the world?

- What keeps me from extending God's reign to others who seem so difficult?

- Do I judge by appearance and hearsay?

- God's Spirit rests in me. As a follower of Jesus do I see myself as responsible to live in hope and work for the establishment of God's reign?

- What good news about God's fidelity have I refused to believe? Why?

- What change must I make in my life to advance God's loving presence each day?

Celebration of Reconciliation

Sisters and brothers, let us remember how God longs to come into our lives. Let us kneel and ask forgiveness for our refusal to receive and extend God's reign in our hearts and in our world.

All: I confess to our saving God,
to all whom I have influenced toward evil,
and especially to everyone here,
that I have sinned in my thoughts and actions.
I ask Mary, the mother of our church,
all the holy ones who have lived to establish God's reign,
especially John the Baptist,
and everyone here,
to pray for me
for healing and conversion.

Song of contrition

Lord's Prayer

Let us ask forgiveness so that the reign of God may come more fully this Christmas time.

All: Our Father, who art in heaven, . . .

God,
you who are justice and peace,
free us from all sin.

Help us to announce your coming.

We ask this through Jesus, your Son and our Savior.

All: Amen.

Silent prayer/reflection for conversion of heart

Proclamation of praise for God's mercy: *Psalm 18:2–4, 17, 20, 28, 31–32, 36–37, 47*

(stand)

Group 1

I love you, O Lord, my strength,
> O Lord, my rock, my fortress, my deliverer.

My God, my rock of refuge,
> my shield, the horn of my salvation, my stronghold!

Praised be the Lord, I exclaim,
> and I am safe from my enemies.

Group 2

He reached out from on high and grasped me;
He set me free in the open,
> and rescued me, because he loves me.

For lowly people you save
> but haughty eyes you bring low;

Group 1

God's way is unerring,
> the promise of the Lord is fire-tried;
> he is a shield to all who take refuge in him.

For who is God except the Lord?
> Who is a rock, save our God?

Group 2

You have given me your saving shield;
> your right hand has upheld me,
> and you have stooped to make me great.

You made room for my steps;
> unwavering was my stride.

All: **The Lord live! And blessed be my Rock!**
Extolled be God my savior.

Concluding prayer of thanksgiving

Lord Jesus Christ,
You have extended your mercy to us,
strengthened us with your love,
renewed us in the hope of your continual coming.

We rejoice in your presence with us now.

Help us persevere in loving and forgiving one another and ourselves,
so we become ever clearer signs of your reign in our world.

You who are present now,
and continue to come until the fullness of time,
forever and ever.

All: **Amen.**

Conclusion

Blessing

> May the Father bless us,
> for we are created in the image of the Savior.

All: **Amen.**

> May the Son come to help us, for we extend his reign through our
> baptismal commitment.

All: **Amen.**

> May the Spirit be with us,
> for we are the dwelling places of the blossom of the root of Jesse.

All: **Amen.**

Dismissal

> The LORD has freed us from our sins.
> Let us go in peace.

Response: Thanks be to God.

Closing song

Resources
The Coming of God's Reign—Advent, Cycle A

Scripture Reflection Suggestions for *Is 11:1–10* and *Mt 11:2–11*

The focus of this celebration is the reign of God. Advent can be for us a checking of the strength of this phenomena in our own hearts and in our own world. Some ideas to reflect on are the following:

1. Baptism as our invitation and responsibility to be prophets and proclaimers of the reign of God in a more significant way than John the Baptist (*Mt 11:11*)

2. The signs Jesus identified as showing that the reign of God had come: the blind seeing, cripples walking, lepers cured, the deaf hearing, the dead raised, the poor hearing the good news (*Mt 11:4–5*)

3. Contemporary situations, especially local and national ones, that challenge our baptismal call to justice and peace

4. Dominant scriptural images/ideas of the readings

    a. Shoot from the stump of Jesse—new life, growth (*Is 11:1*)

    b. Wolf/lamb, leopard/kid, etc.—peace and mutual support (*Is 11:6–8*)

    c. Justice and faithfulness, not appearance and hearsay, as the criteria for judgment of those who are genuinely working to establish God's reign (*Is 11:3, 5*)

Music Suggestions

Opening and closing songs

"The Coming of Our God," Anonymous (*People's Mass Book*)

"I Lift Up My Soul," by Tim Manion (*Glory and Praise*)

"City of God," by Dan Schutte, S.J. (*Glory and Praise*)

"Let There Be Peace On Earth," by Sy Miller and Jill Jackson (*Gather to Remember*)

Responsorial psalm (alternate version which is sung)

"Justice Shall Flourish," by Timothy M. Schoenbachler. (*Gather to Remember*)

Song of contrition

"Dwelling Place," by John Foley, S.J. (*Glory and Praise*)

"Amazing Grace," (*People's Mass Book*)

"Pardon Your People," by Carey Landry (*Glory and Praise*)

"Jesus Heal Us," by David Haas (*Who Calls You By Name*, Vol I. G.I.A. Publications)

Reflective music

> *Harboring the Holy* by Robert M. Hutmacher, OFM
> (G.I.A. Publications)
>
> *Free Fall* by Patrick Loomis (Oregon Catholic Press Publications)

Environment suggestions

After a while, finding a new way to present the traditional Advent wreath can be challenging. Consider this idea for use as Advent environment, not only for this penitential service, but for the worship space for the entire season. Since variety refreshes prayer as well as instructs, use the familiar imagery of the stump of Jesse as found in the *first reading*. (*Is 11:1–10*)

Place a tree stump of significant size where it can be seen by the worshipping community. (Some good ways to locate a tree stump are to contact members of the faith community who may have cut down some trees lately, or to call a local tree trimming company and ask them to donate one, or to inquire at your local landscaper or nursery.) Elevating it on a table, which may need a cloth cover, is often practical. It is helpful if the stump has two or three places where sizeable limbs have been cut off. The stump's size should not overshadow the altar.

Adorn it with the traditional Advent candles (three dark blue, or gray, and one white, or three red violet and one pink) and some greenery, evergreen branches, and holly. Light the candles as usual during the weeks of Advent.

All of the traditional symbolism will still apply except the wreath's circle. Instead, the faith community can recall the promise fulfilled through Jesse, David's father, and its fulfillment through us as we continue to establish God's reign in our time. Use of either symbol recalls God's endless love.

Further suggestions

1. Lights could be lowered to create a reflective mood.

2. Using a portable microphone, various voices could read each section of the *examination of conscience* from the assembly, highlighting our common need for reconciliation.

3. To promote a prayerful atmosphere, reflective music is encouraged during the *examination of conscience* and during the *silent prayer/reflection for conversion of heart*. Enlisting music ministers is always preferred, but if this is not possible, suggestions for some appropriate music tapes or compact discs are listed in the music suggestions section.

Waiting in Joyful Hope

Gathering

Opening song

Greeting

In the name of the Father, and of the Son, and of the Holy Spirit.

May the grace, mercy, and peace of our loving God be with you.

All: **And also with you.**

Introduction

Waiting is the work of Advent. But what is our waiting about? Jesus came long ago, and we believe that we have forgiveness for our sins.

Our waiting has a distant focus and is one firmly marked with hope. We await the new heavens and the new earth, the time when the justice of God will reside in all people's hearts. Let us pray now with and for each other in this time of waiting.

Opening prayer

Let us pray. *(period of silence)*

Patient God,
you want all people to be saved,
but that is as much our choice as yours.
You ask us to stay awake to your coming
but we do not easily recognize you
because we are often distracted
by our own concerns.

Give us the grace to know
that our days are the waiting time
in which we welcome or reject your love.

Help us to embrace our role
of witnessing to your compassionate and saving presence
among all people,
now and in the time to come.

We ask this through Jesus, our Lord and Redeemer.

All: **Amen.**

Celebration of the Word of God

First Reading: *2 Pt 3:8–14*

Response

> *(followed by a brief period of silence)*

Gospel acclamation

Gospel: *Mk 13:33–37*

Scripture reflection

Examination of conscience

> *(All kneel)*

> While we wait we strive to grow in the hope that our loving God has held out to us in the coming of Jesus. We look into our hearts now for evidence that we are being God's hopeful people.

> - How do I watch for God's presence in my days?
> - Am I a joyful, positive person, expecting God to place things in my life that draw us closer together?
> - When do I take time to reflect on the experiences of the day in order to open myself to God's presence?
> - In or on what do I rely for happiness and security? Success? Money? Possessions? Control?
>
> - Am I a person of hope? Do I actively hand on the best of my gift of life to others around me, especially the children?
> - Do I believe that God will forgive and forget my weaknesses and sins?
> - Where in my life do I need God's forgiveness most?
> - Do I trust that God is always with me, leading me to the fullest meaning of life, in every circumstance I experience?
>
> - How do I do the work entrusted to me so as to be ready for God's arrival?
> - How do I see the face of God in my loved ones, my parishioners, my neighbors and co-workers?
> - In these daily contacts what do I say or do that communicates the values of Jesus?
> - How does God speak to me in the homeless, the welfare recipient, the abused, the physically and mentally handicapped, the jobless?
> - Am I aware that caring for their needs is a way to prepare myself for God's coming?
> - What have I done recently to help the struggling poor?

- Do I have more than I need for essential living, for the future security of my family, for safety, health, and happiness?
- Am I dominated by the excess materialism and values of television shows and commercials and spend my time and efforts to achieve that style of life?
- Where do I seek support to live a life based on the belief that Jesus is coming again?

Celebration of Reconciliation

Let us confess our sins together.

All: **I confess to our patient God,
and to all here present
that I have sinned
in my thoughts, words, and deeds.**

**I ask Mary, all the angels and saints,
everyone I have known, both living and dead,
and particularly everyone here
to forgive me
and pray for me.**

Litany of contrition

(All stand)

In a spirit of repentance and sincere hope let us ask God to forgive our sins and make us people who joyfully look for God's coming.

That we may have watchful spirits to avoid squandering your gifts of time and life,

All: **Come, help us and forgive us.**

That we may have trusting hearts to believe in your presence and your coming,

All: **Come, help us and forgive us.**

That we may have hope to end the despair and faithlessness of our time,

All: **Come, help us and forgive us.**

That we may have your peace to welcome you in all we meet,

All: **Come, help us and forgive us.**

That we may be drawn to you, O God, and away from the passing attractions around us each day,

All: **Come, help us and forgive us.**

That we may live simply and share without judging,

All: **Come, help us and forgive us.**

That we may persevere in placing your saving love at the center of our lives,

All: **Come, help us and forgive us.**

That we may be renewed in patience and prayer as we remember your promise to give us new heavens and a new earth,

All: **Come, help us and forgive us.**

Lord's Prayer

Let us pray together for forgiveness and protection in the words Jesus taught us.

All: **Our Father, who art in heaven, . . .**

God,
you who wait for us to receive your love,
pardon our offenses
and fill us with your peace.

Help us to wait for you in joyful hope.

We ask this through Jesus our Redeemer.

All: **Amen.**

Silent prayer/reflection for conversion of heart

Proclamation of praise for God's mercy

(stand)

Concluding prayer of thanksgiving

God of all time,
you are the source of our true hope.

Your word has revealed to us
that we wait for each other.

We thank you for your forgiveness
and ask your help to welcome your great love
during all the days to come.

Make us people of joy and promise
so your saving grace is known to all.

We ask this through Jesus Christ our Lord.

All: **Amen.**

Conclusion

Blessing

May God, who always waits for our coming, bless us with hope.

All: **Amen.**

May Jesus Christ, the Son, who will return one day, bless us with perseverance.

All: **Amen.**

May the Holy Spirit, who lives in our hearts, bless us with joy.

All: **Amen.**

Dismissal

Let us go in peace to love and serve God.

All: **Thanks be to God.**

Closing song

Resources
Waiting in Joyful Hope—Advent, Cycle B

Scripture reflection suggestions for *2 Pt 3:8–14* and *Mk 13:33–37*

This celebration focuses on waiting and on persevering, joyful hope. The following are possible ideas for reflection.

1. While we wait and watch and stay on guard for the Lord's coming (*Mk 13:33*), it is much more significant to believe and trust that God has been waiting and watching for us. With God there is no time, "...a day is like a thousand years, and a thousand years are like a day" (*2 Pt 3:8–9*). The Lord will return when we are ready to receive that glorious presence. Part of that return happens now in this celebration. Do I realize that God is waiting for me, right now?

2. The hallmark of a Christian person is hope. "What we are waiting for, relying on his promises, is the new heavens and new earth, where uprightness will be at home" (*2 Pt 3:13*). We have every reason to move into the days ahead with confidence and peace and life-giving energy because our sins have been forgiven. They have no power over us in any permanent way. No matter *what* happens our life is secure. Our greatest sorrows, tragedies, and obstacles are understood by Jesus and put into perspective for us by his love. In my daily Christian living I am called to witness this hope so that others can be in touch with God's presence in their hearts and lives. Am I a person of hope in our world?

3. It seems that many people are not consciously waiting for God because their concept of God is not a positive one. How we wait is highly colored by our understanding of who and what we wait for. Reflecting on the images of God that we hold is another homily idea. When we think of Jesus as the human expression of God, we can begin to have a true picture of God because that image is grounded in the Christian Scriptures. Watching Jesus as he interacts with others, listening to his words, reflecting on his feelings, contemplating his relationships with the Father and Spirit are ways we can come to know God in human form. This is the real God for whom we wait, and thus our Advent waiting takes on authentic Christian characteristics developing a mature spirituality. How do I wait? Who is my God?

Music suggestions

Opening and closing songs

"Blest Be the Lord," by Dan Schutte, S.J. (*Glory and Praise*)

"Come, O Long-Awaited Savior," by William Walker (*People's Mass Book*)

"Dwelling Place," by John Foley, S.J. (*Glory and Praise*)

"Patience People," by John Foley, S.J. (*Glory and Praise*)

"Sing Out His Goodness," by Darryl Ducote (*Glory and Praise*)

Response

"I Lift Up My Soul," by Tim Manion (*Glory and Praise*)

"Isaiah 49," by Reverend Carey Landry (*Glory and Praise*)

"To You, O Lord," by Marty Haugen (*Gather To Remember*)

"Wait for the Lord," by Jacques Berthier (*Songs and Prayers from Taizé*, G.I.A. Publications)

Gospel acclamation

"Alleluia," by Jan M. Vermulst (*People's Mass Book*)

"We Remember," (refrain only) by Marty Haugen (*Music Issue 1995*)

Proclamation of praise

"Sing a New Song," by Dan Schutte, S.J. (*Glory and Praise*)

"Glory and Praise to Our God," by Dan Schutte, S.J. (*Glory and Praise*)

Reflective music

"Ode to Joy," by Daniel Kobialka (*Sun Space*, Li-Sem Enterprises) Pachelbel Canon in D Major.

"Hallelujah Chorus" of Handel's *Messiah*

Environment suggestions

1. A way to vary the Advent environment for the whole season, and also to make it appropriate for this penitential service, would be to prepare a wall hanging (or set of hangings) with symbols of the new heavens and the new earth. The graphic associated with the accompanying service suggests simple buildings that symbolize the new Jerusalem. The visual of this city is a practical, specific design from which to start. The Advent colors of red, violet (predominantly), gray, white and black would be effective. Artists, sewers, and craft persons (weavers, too!), men and women, all could assist with design, fabric selection, and hanging.

    If this option is used, a brief explanation of the hangings can be given to the people to facilitate their understanding of the community's focus for this season. This long-range look at the coming of the Lord has not been presented to us very often. Yet, it does give a perspective on our identity, particularly in these times of instantaneous results.

2. Another environment idea, a variation from the Advent wreath that could be used for the entire season as well as this penitential service, is the Jesse Tree. This backward glance at our family faith history could serve to remind the community of our patient, continuing stance of waiting and watching. We are waiting like priests, prophets, holy people, and kings of old for the second coming of the Savior. Again, some explanation to the community would be appropriate.

Other groups in the community may be interested in making the symbols, or providing the explanation of them for the larger community, or putting up and taking down the tree. Do you have Bible study groups, or other adult education groups, small Christian communities, a worship commission with small committees, junior high religion programs? Increasing others' participation in group worship builds a community of knowledge, ownership, service, faith, and hope.

Further suggestions

1. One of the suggested responses to follow the first reading is the Taizé "Wait for the Lord." In addition to the tape, words and music can be found in the book, *Songs and Prayers from Taizé*. The refrain can easily be taught to and sung by the assembly while a cantor or choir can sing the verses.

2. The *examination of conscience* can be read by various individuals, men and women, of all adult ages. Some readers could speak from their places in the community (using a portable microphone). This variation recalls that everyone needs forgiveness and reconciliation.

3. In order to aid in personal centering, reflection music is suggested during the time of *silent prayer/reflection for conversion of heart*. Music ministers often have a repertoire that will meet this need. Live music is always preferred. However, there are recorded suggestions here if music ministers are not available. The classical selections "Ode to Joy" by Beethoven and the "Hallelujah Chorus" from Handel's *Messiah* are best if the arrangement is a slow one. Daniel Kobialka's *Sun Space* tape has a good example of the "Ode to Joy."

Bringing God to Birth

Gathering

Opening song

Greeting

Faith, mercy, and peace to you from God, our Immanuel.

Response: And also with you.

Introduction

We are the most blessed of people. Our God once took on human flesh and lived on our earth because an ordinary woman lived her life with extraordinary faith.

The way God has left it is that God asks to be born over and over, but in us. And so we are gifted with faith and called to live it, ~~like Mary,~~ in a profound way.

Let us, ~~with Mary as our guide,~~ look at our lives and our faith to see how significantly we have brought God into our world.

Opening prayer

Let us pray. *(period of silence)*

God, our Immanuel,
we believe you are alive in us
because of our faith in Jesus, your son.

But our faith is often dulled,
buried under circumstances
that lead to selfishness, oppression, and even violence.

We come to ask for healing and help.

Give us deeper trust in you,
to act in new ways,
that we may bring you to a needy world.

We ask this through Christ our Lord.

Response: Amen.

Celebration of the Word of God

First reading: *Is 7:14*

Response

> *(followed by a brief period of silence)*

Second reading: *Gal 4:4–7*

Gospel acclamation

Gospel: *Lk 1:39–45*

> *(followed by a brief period of silence)*

Examination of conscience

(all kneel)

> Mary's faith grew deeper as the events of her life unfolded. Scripture tells us she reflected on her daily life patterns.

- Do I foster the habit of remembering God is Immanuel, "God with us?"
- How do I listen for God's voice, look for signs of God's action in the people and circumstances around me?
- How willing am I to be open to God's invitation to grow in faith?
- What does God seem to be asking of me now?
- Do I ask God to increase my faith?

> *(period of silence)*

Mary, wellspring of peace	**Be our guide.**
Model of strength	**Be our guide.**
Model of gentleness	**Be our guide.**
Model of trust	**Be our guide.**
Model of courage	**Be our guide.**
Model of patience	**Be our guide.**
Model of risk	**Be our guide.**
Model of openness	**Be our guide.**
Model of perseverance	**Be our guide.**

As a spouse and parent Mary faced many unforeseen events in her family relationships. She believed God would help her give love and life to those nearest her each time a new challenge in their relationship arose.

- What circumstance in my family life is most difficult for me now?

- Do I respond by condemning, or with violence?

- How could I give life and love in that circumstance?

- How clear to those with whom I live is my example of faith?

- When I experience no evidence that faith will make a difference, do I, like Mary, continue to hope and act in hope?

(period of silence)

Mother of the liberator	**Pray for us.**
Mother of the homeless	**Pray for us.**
Mother of the dying	**Pray for us.**
Mother of the nonviolent	**Pray for us.**
Widowed mother	**Pray for us.**
Mother of a political prisoner	**Pray for us.**
Mother of the condemned	**Pray for us.**
Mother of the executed criminal	**Pray for us.**

Mary's faith in God's ways led her to stand outside accepted circles socially, politically, and even at times, religiously. She was the peaceful, strong, compassionate presence that supported others, even the apostles, when human structures had to change. She trusted God to be at work in very radical situations.

- How accepting am I of others who are different, who are marginalized, who seek sanctuary for political, social, or religious reasons?

- What attitudes grow deeply in my heart that make me a slave to the law for my own security?

- What fears keep me from reaching out to the oppressed?

- How would I act if I really believed that I could call God "Abba," "Daddy," and depend on that relationship as warm, stable, and life-giving?

- Is there a current situation that calls me to respond to others in need because of my faith?

(period of silence)

Oppressed woman	**Lead us to life.**
Liberator of the oppressed	**Lead us to life.**
Marginalized woman	**Lead us to life.**
Comforter of the afflicted	**Lead us to life.**
Cause of our joy	**Lead us to life.**
Sign of contradiction	**Lead us to life.**
Breaker of bondage	**Lead us to life.**
Political refugee	**Lead us to life.**
Seeker of sanctuary	**Lead us to life.**
First disciple	**Lead us to life.**
Sharer in Christ's ministry	**Lead us to life.**
Participant in Christ's passion	**Lead us to life.**
Seeker of God's will	**Lead us to life.**
Witness to Christ's resurrection	**Lead us to life.**

Mary lived with God as the center of her life. She continually tried to learn about God and to make her life's decisions in the light of what God would want.

- What is my understanding of God?
- Is my image of God in harmony with the way Jesus describes God?
- What am I doing to get to know God better? When do we talk?
- What are the signs that our relationship is growing?
- How do I invite God into the decisions I make?

  (period of silence)

Woman of mercy	**Empower us.**
Woman of faith	**Empower us.**
Woman of contemplation	**Empower us.**
Woman of vision	**Empower us.**
Woman of wisdom and understanding	**Empower us.**
Woman of grace and truth	**Empower us.**
Woman, pregnant with hope	**Empower us.**
Woman, centered in God	**Empower us.**

Celebration of Reconciliation

Sisters and brothers, let us confess our sins.

All: **I confess to God,**
and to all of you, my sisters and brothers,
that I have sinned
and not always lived by my covenant of faith.

I ask Mary, courageous and compassionate woman of faith,
all holy people of God,
and particularly you, sisters and brothers,
to pray to God for me.

Lord's Prayer

Using the words of Mary's son, let us pray together for forgiveness and protection from evil.

All: **Our Father, who art in heaven . . .**
Merciful God,
forgive us
for refusing to allow you
to live more fully in us.

Bring us to deeper faith and trust in your love.

We ask this in Jesus' name.

All: **Amen.**

Silent prayer/reflection for conversion of heart

Proclamation of praise for God's mercy

(stand)

Concluding prayer of thanksgiving

Faithful Immanuel,
we know again your love and mercy.

Like Mary, we opened to your presence
and have been filled with your life.

Continue to bless us with this receptivity
so our actions give proof
that you are truly present
to all in our needy world.

We ask this through Mary's son.

All: **Amen.**

Conclusion

Blessing

> May God
> the Creator, Redeemer, and Sanctifier
> bless us
> and bring us to deeper faith,
> as did the Holy Spirit for Mary.

All: **Amen.**

Dismissal

> We believe God frees us from our sin. We are truly blessed. Let us go in peace.

All: **Thanks be to God.**

Closing song

Litany invocations are taken from "Litany of Mary of Nazareth," *Pax Christi*, Erie, PA.

Resources
Bringing God to Birth—Advent, Cycle C

Scripture reflection suggestion

In this service the *Litany of Mary of Nazareth* serves to "break open" the word of God. Therefore, a scripture reflection is not needed.

Music suggestions

Opening and closing songs

"O Mary of All Women," by Edward L. Throm (*Peoples Mass Book*)

"Emanuel," by Tim Manion (*Glory and Praise*)

"Hail Mary: Gentle Woman," by Carey Landry (*Glory and Praise*)

"Sing Out His Goodness," by Darryl Ducote (*Glory and Praise*)

Response

"O Come, O Come Emmanuel"

"Mary the Dawn," by Justin Mulcahy, C.P. (*Peoples Mass Book*)

"Remember Your Love," by Darryl Ducote and Gary Daigle (*Glory and Praise*)

Gospel acclamation

"Alleluia," by Robert F. Twynham (*Peoples Mass Book*)

"Alleluia," Chant (*Peoples Mass Book*)

Proclamation of praise

"My Soul Rejoices," by Gary Ault et al (*Glory and Praise*)

A recited "Magnificat," your choice of translation.

Reflective music

Sun Space by Daniel Kobialka (Li-Sem Enterprises)

Comfort Zone by Steven Halpern (Halpern Sounds)

Environment suggestions

1. Mary is a predominant Advent figure. Who more than she waited for the coming of the Savior? Who more than she brought him into the world? Who more than she contributed to the establishment of the new covenant present now until Jesus returns again? It is fitting that she be significantly incorporated into our Advent liturgical environment.

   A suggestion for the environment for this penitential service would be to adapt the Advent wreath colors to reflect the contemplative, quiet, waiting season of winter and the traditional "Mary" colors. In doing this, nothing more would be needed for this celebration. Use all dark blue candles, or three dark blue candles and one white candle for the wreath. A variation would be to use four white or cream colored candles with dark blue bows or ribbon decoratively placed through the wreath. Simplicity in its design is essential. The wreath may be hung on the wall, suspended from the ceiling, or mounted on a stand. It should not overpower the altar or ambo.

2. A second idea is to highlight a statue, window, or icon of Mary that is already a part of your worship space. Lighting, hanging fabric, and simple greenery are all ways to enhance this spot and focus attention on Mary for Advent. Perhaps four candles could be included in this environment and lit as the weeks advance. Original, short prayers could be written that highlight the Advent experience as Mary lived it, and we, the Church, are striving to live it. These could be prayed each of the four weeks as the candles are lit.

Further suggestions

1. The *examination of conscience* could be read by a lector or combination of lectors. This highlights the need for reconciliation within the community.

   The presider could also read the examination.

2. The presider could lead the *Litany of Mary of Nazareth,* or it could be recited by the assembly in choirs, that is alternating sides.

   The litany could also be chanted by a choir or cantor with the assembly responding. The simple chant mode of the Litany of the Saints could be adapted here.

3. Reflective music is encouraged during the time of *silent prayer/reflection for conversion of heart.* Enlisting music ministers is always preferred, but if this is not possible, suggestions for some appropriate music tapes or compact discs are listed in the preceding music suggestions section.

   Consider also the possibility of congregational singing interspersed with reflective listening. Songs cited in the music suggestions section could be used in this way.

At Lenten Time

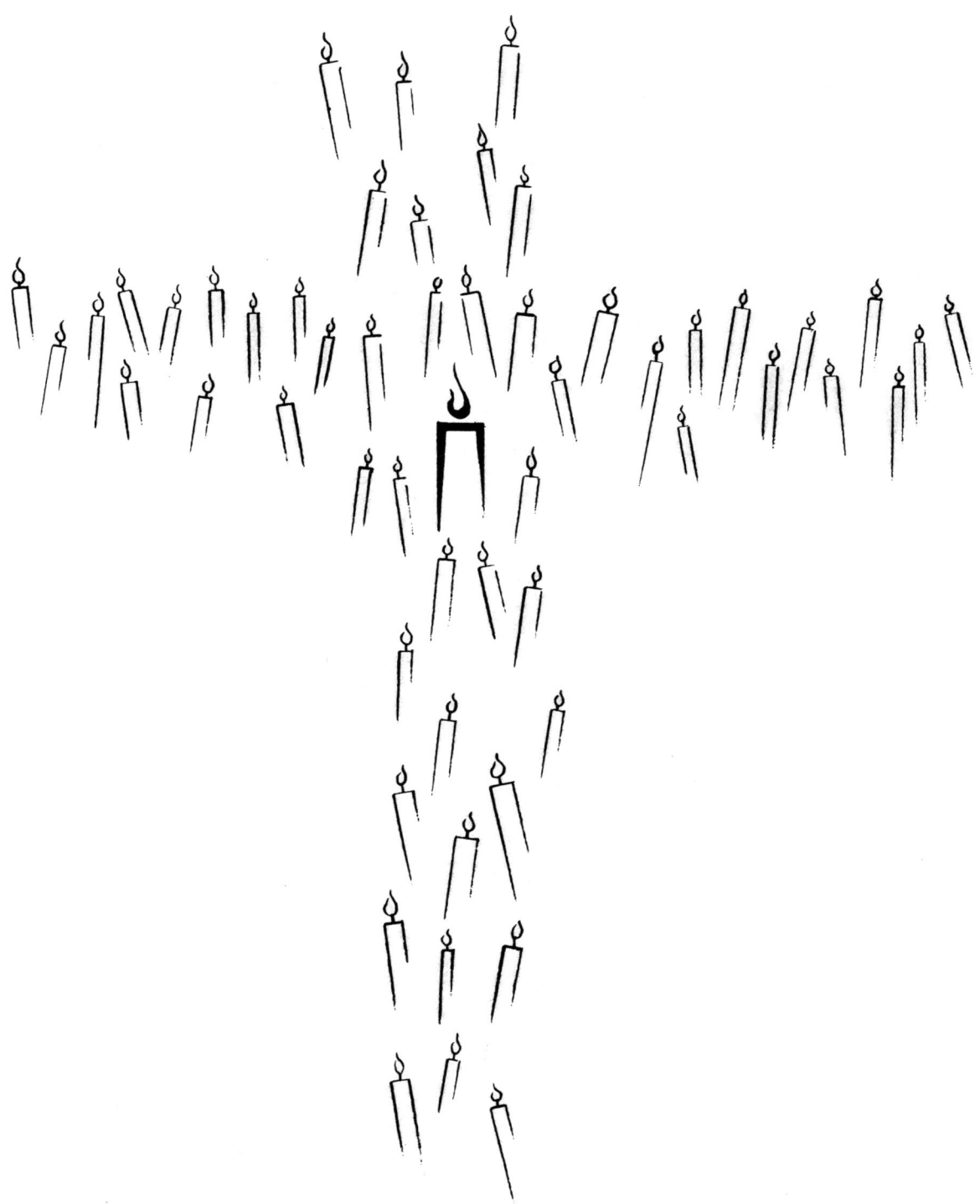

Walking in the Light

Gathering

Opening song

Greeting

> May the light of the Lord dispel the darkness in our hearts and renew in us peace.

Response: Amen.

Introduction

> We are a community begun in light, the light of the resurrection. We each received that light at the time of our baptism. We gather now to consider how brightly that flame is burning in our thoughts, words, and actions.
>
> Let us ask the Lord for hearts filled with sincere repentance.
>
> *(period of silence)*

Opening prayer

> Lord of light,
>
> God of our salvation,
>
> We come to acknowledge the darkness
> that has entered our lives.
>
> Help us to celebrate your love and mercy,
> so that the light of your presence
> may shine brightly in the world through us.
>
> We ask this in Jesus' name.

Response: Amen.

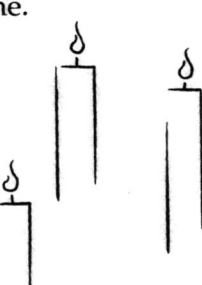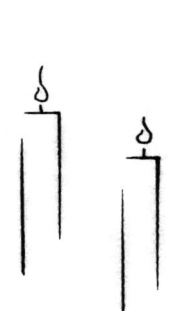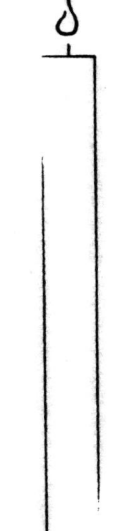

Celebration of the Word of God

First reading: *Eph 5:8–20*

> *(period of silence)*

Responsorial psalm: *Ps 27:1, 7–14*

> **Response: The Lord is my light and my salvation; whom should I fear?**
>
> > Hear, O LORD, the sound of my call;
> > > have pity on me, and answer me.
> > Of you my heart speaks; you my glance seeks;
> > > your presence, O LORD, I seek.
>
> **Response**
> > Hide not your face from me;
> > > do not in anger repel your servant.
> > You are my helper: cast me not off;
> > > forsake me not, O God my savior.
>
> **Response**
> > Though my father and mother forsake me,
> > > yet will the LORD receive me.
>
> **Response**
> > Show me, O LORD, your way,
> > > and lead me on a level path,
> > because of my adversaries.
> > Give me not up to the wishes of my foes;
> > > for false witnesses have risen up against me,
> > > and such as breathe out violence.
>
> **Response**
> > I believe that I shall see the bounty of the LORD
> > > in the land of the living.
> > Wait for the LORD with courage;
> > > be stouthearted, and wait for the LORD.

Gospel acclamation

> **Glory and praise to you, LORD Jesus Christ!**
>
> > I am the light of the world.
> > Those who follow me will have the light of life (*Jn 8:12*).
>
> **Glory and praise to you, Lord Jesus Christ!**

Gospel: *Mt 20:30–34*

Scripture reflection

Examination of Conscience

(kneel)

Where is the darkness in my relationship with God?

- Is it in the lack of time I take to listen consciously to God?

- Is it in the opportunities I choose that allow me to ignore God's invitation to deeper faith and commitment?

- Is it in my own unwillingness to remember God's presence on a daily basis?

- Is the darkness because I fear God?

- Is the darkness because I feel God to be far away or not interested in me?

Where is the darkness in my relationship with myself?

- Is it in my inability to befriend myself, to accept who I am? Do I want, plan, and pray for the continuing holiness God makes possible for me?

- Is it in my addictions—to appearance, to status, to security, to pleasure, to control?

- Is the darkness because I do not believe that I am infinitely lovable in God's eyes?

- Is the darkness because I do not truly recognize that Jesus wants me, needs me, to carry the light of his love to others?

Where is the darkness in my relationships with others?

- Is it in a lack of concern and commitment to the larger good—my extended family, my parish, my neighborhood, my job?

- Is it in a lack of honest understanding and action about the inequalities that cause suffering among races, countries, sexes, and social groups?

- Is the darkness because I genuinely feel that others can make it on their own if they really want to?

- Is the darkness because I do not have a constant, grateful spirit, but believe I have earned my own way through life?

Celebration of Reconciliation

Let us confess our sins and pray for God's light.

All:　**We confess to you, almighty God,**
here in each other's presence,
that we have brought the darkness of sin
to our world,
and especially to those closest to us.

We ask for the prayers of all the angels and saints,
the compassion and love of your Son,
and your mercy and light.

Song of contrition

Lord's Prayer

Jesus has taught us how to ask for forgiveness in his prayer
to the Father.
Let us together pray.

All:　**Our Father, who art in heaven, . . .**

Saving God,
brightness of truth and justice and holiness,
forgive us for preferring darkness
to the marvelous light of your love.

Take away our blindness,
and strengthen us
to make the most of your opportunities of grace,
so we may be your light for our sisters and brothers.

We ask this through Jesus Christ,
who, with the Holy Spirit, is the light of the world.

All:　**Amen.**

Silent prayer/reflection for conversion of heart

Proclamation of praise for God's mercy: *Ps 32:1–7, 10–11*

Once you were in darkness, but now you are light in the Lord.
Let us praise and thank God.

**Response: Happy is he whose fault is taken away,
whose sin is covered.**

Happy the man to whom the LORD imputes not guilt,
in whose spirit there is no guile.
As long as I would not speak, my bones wasted away
with my groaning all the day,

Response

For day and night your hand was heavy upon me;
my strength was dried up as by the heat of summer.
Then I acknowledged my sin to you,
my guilt I covered not.

Response

I said, "I confess my faults to the LORD,"
and you took away the guilt of my sin.
For this shall every faithful man pray to you
in time of stress.
Though deep waters overflow,
they shall not reach him.

Response

You are my shelter; from distress you will preserve me;
with glad cries of freedom you will ring me round.
Many are the sorrows of the wicked,
but kindness surrounds him who trusts in the LORD.
Be glad in the LORD and rejoice, you just;
exult, all you upright of heart.

Response

Concluding prayer of thanksgiving

Lord God,
You have rekindled your light in us
through your tender forgiveness
and the unconditional love of Jesus on the cross.

May this love be our strength
to keep your saving light burning.

Help us to bring the light of your presence
to all the world.

We ask this in the name of Jesus, our Lord.

All: Amen.

Conclusion

Blessing

We have been brought out of darkness into God's wonderful light.
May God bless us,
the Creator, the Redeemer, the Sanctifier.

All: **Amen.**

Dismissal

Go in peace, and live as children of the light.

All: **We will indeed!**

Closing song

Resources

Walking in the Light—Lent, Cycle A

Scripture reflection suggestions for *Eph 5:8–20* and *Mt 20:30–34*

This celebration considers the opposite forces of light and darkness that every baptized person must face on a daily basis. Making choices is an essential part of the conversion process, which is our Lenten journey. This experience of struggle is where we meet the Lord. The *scripture reflection* will affect the hearts and minds of those assembled if it is based in the reality of this struggle. Reflecting on the experiences of life can be spiritually powerful. Some suggested ideas are listed below.

1. In the gospel Jesus asks the question, "What do you want me to do for you?" (*Mt 20:32*). Before I can answer Jesus, I must be in touch with and name my needs. How am I needy? What controls my life that makes me blind? Naming my blindness and my needs allows me to talk with Jesus and answer Jesus' question.

2. Who has not been disturbed by the events of the evening news or the daily paper? Bombings, atrocities committed against children, systematic destruction of nations, and the dissolution of family identity are all daily occurrences—". . . the days are evil" (*Eph 5:16*). The light of God's love is not present in many people's lives. What is lacking that allows evil to have control?

   Reflecting on my personal responsibility to struggle with and oppose the evils that become everyday occurrences opens me to the blindness I have within. How do I confront evil when it touches my daily life? How courageous am I in teaching and modeling the values of Jesus, especially when they involve personal sacrifice for the good of the whole?

Music suggestions

Opening and closing songs

> "Awake, O Sleeper," by Mike Balhoff, Darryl Ducote, and Gary Daigle (*Glory and Praise*)
>
> "God of Day and God of Darkness," Text by Marty Haugen, music from the Sacred Harp (*Music Issue 1995*)
>
> "Son of David," by John Foley, S.J. (*Glory and Praise*)
>
> "Christ Will Be Your Light," by David Haas (*Who Calls You By Name*, Vol. I, G.I.A. Publications)
>
> "He Healed the Darkness of My Mind," by David Haas (*Who Calls You By Name*, Vol. I, G. I. A. Publications)
>
> "The Lord Is My Life," by Michael Joncas (*God of Life and of the Living*, G.I.A. Publications)
>
> "Here I Am, Lord,"—especially verses 1 and 2—by Dan Schutte, S.J. (*Glory and Praise*)

Responsorial psalm

"On Eagle's Wings," by Michael Joncas (*Glory and Praise*) (alternate suggestion to *Psalm 27* in printed service)

"Open My Eyes," by Jesse Manibusan (*Light of Christ*, Oregon Catholic Press Publications)

Gospel acclamation

"Light of Christ," by Rufino Zaragoza, O.F.M. Conv. (*Light of Christ*, Oregon Catholic Press Publications)

Song of contrition

"God of All Mercy," vs. 1–3, by David Haas (*Who Calls You By Name*, Vol. I, G.I.A. Publications)

"Jesus, Heal Us," by David Haas (*Who Calls You By Name*, Vol. I, G. I. A. Publications)

Reflection music

Dawn—Extended Play—especially side 1—by Steven Halpern (Halpern Sounds)

Titania The Fairy Queen by Mike Rowland (Antiquity Records)

Environment suggestions

1. The easiest way to provide a supportive environment for this penitential service is with the use of the lighting already available in the worship space. Begin the service with normal lighting. After the *scripture reflection*, as the *examination of conscience* begins, gradually dim or reduce the lighting. Keep this subdued and darker atmosphere through the time of *silent prayer/reflection for conversion of heart*. The lack of clarity and joy, the limitations that sin brings, can more easily be felt. If reflective music is also played, as suggested, this quiet, nondistracting environment should foster prayerfulness.

   As the *proclamation of praise for God's mercy* begins, gradually increase the lighting until the *concluding prayer*, when the lights can be at their maximum. At the *conclusion*, the community is sent forth in the fullness of light.

2. The focus of Lent is conversion. Therefore, many worshipping communities use the element of sand as part of an environment, most especially in the area where the people enter the church. Sand recalls the desert, a traditional place of conversion.

   If you incorporate a desert place in your gathering area for Lent, sand could be aesthetically placed for this penitential service (in rectangular flower boxes possibly) in the form of a cross, before the ambo or at the head of the center aisle if it does not intrude on the space of the altar table. The sand cross must be visible and accessible to the community. (Elevating it and tilting it forward is very helpful.) The cross should be large enough to permit each person to place a taper candle in the sand.

Purple fabric may be needed to call attention to the cross and to add beauty and simplicity to the containers. A proportionately large plain candle can be placed in the center of the cross.

Taper candles can be placed in simple baskets in proximity to the sand cross.

As the gospel acclamation is prayed the large candle, already placed in the sand cross, is lit. After the period of *silent prayer/reflection for conversion of heart*, members of the assembly can individually take a taper and light it from the large, lit candle. The taper is then placed in the sand, forming a cross of light. This penitential service has been our contact with Jesus, the light of the world. We once again see as Jesus sees. With this ritual gesture we affirm the cross to be the light of life.

Further suggestions

1. The *responsorial psalm, Ps 27*, printed in the service, can be led by a lector with the assembly reciting the response, or the alternate sung responses, given in music resources, can be used. If one of the latter is chosen, the *responsorial psalm* as printed can be eliminated from the copies made for the assembly.

2. The *gospel acclamation* can be sung to any familiar Lenten melody, or simply recited by the assembly. A cantor can chant the verse, or a lector can proclaim it. Note also the alternate sung chant in the resource section.

3. If the sand cross and tapers are going to be the environment for the service, one of the lectors can light the large candle when the *gospel acclamation* is prayed.

4. See the Advent penitential services for suggestions to present the *examination of conscience*.

5. Reflection music greatly aids personal prayer during the time of *silent prayer/reflection for conversion of heart*. If musicians are not available, the reflection tapes suggested on these resource pages can meet this need.

6. The *proclamation of praise for God's mercy* is a community experience. It can be prayed in choirs (side to side), with half the assembly doing the verses and the other half the response. Or, the verses can be alternated by each half of the assembly with everyone praying the response. Or, a lector or lectors can lead the verses and the assembly pray the response.

Keeping the Covenant

Gathering

Opening song

Greeting

> We gather to celebrate God's fidelity to the covenant we share. May God's love and peace be with you.

> **Response: And also with you.**

Introduction

> God never stops calling us to love. In Moses' time, God gave the law to guide the chosen people into more life-giving relationships. When that law became an end in itself, God pledged a new covenant, one that was written on our hearts, not on tablets of stone. We know what is right because God has placed this understanding in our hearts. As we come together, we pray to know how well we have kept our covenant with God.

Opening prayer

> Faithful God,
> You teach us how to live
> and how to love.
>
> You are concerned with people everywhere
> and sent Jesus, your son,
> to be our model in loving.
>
> Help us to open ourselves now,
> in honesty and confidence.
>
> We come to hear your word,
> and choose again
> to live our covenant with you.
>
> We ask this help in Jesus' name.

> **Response: Amen.**

Celebration of the Word of God

First reading: *Jer 31:31–34*

> *(period of silence)*

Responsorial psalm: *Ps 111:2–10*

Response: I will give thanks to the Lord with all my heart

> Great are the works of the LORD,
>> exquisite in all their delights.
>
> Majesty and glory are his work,
>> and his justice endures forever.

Response

> He has won renown for his wondrous deeds;
>> gracious and merciful is the LORD.
>
> He has given food to those who fear him;
>> he will forever be mindful of his covenant.
>
> He has made known to his people the power of his works,
>> giving them the inheritance of the nations.

Response

> The works of his hands are faithful and just;
>> sure are all his precepts,
>
> Reliable forever and ever,
>> wrought in truth and equity.

Response

> He has sent deliverance to his people;
>> he has ratified his covenant forever;
>> holy and awesome is his name.

Response

> The fear of the LORD is the beginning of wisdom;
>> prudent are all who live by it.
>> His praise endures forever.

Response

Gospel acclamation

Glory and praise to you, Lord Jesus Christ!

> God has indeed qualified us as ministers of a new covenant, not of letter but of spirit; for the letter brings death, but the Spirit gives life (*2 Cor 3:6*).

Glory and praise to you, Lord Jesus Christ!

Gospel: *Mk 12:28–34*

Scripture reflection

Examination of Conscience

Let us kneel and recall Jesus' words.

He tells us to love God with our whole heart, our whole soul, our whole mind, and our whole strength (*Mk 12:30*).

- How seriously do I take my covenant with God; how much does that relationship guide all I think, say, and do?

- How do I seek out the guidance of the Holy Spirit as I strive to fulfill my baptismal promises?

- Am I living the old covenant concerned primarily with external standards and not acknowledging the directives of a wise heart?

Jesus tells us to love our neighbor as we do ourselves. (*Mk 12:31*).

- Have I allowed sacrifices and penances to be the measure of my fidelity to God rather than the love of my neighbor?

- How am I striving to live the spirit of the law in my relationships?

- How am I becoming a person of reconciliation?

- What do I do to strengthen the new covenant present in the hearts of those I see each day?

    (period of silence)

Celebration of Reconciliation

Let us acknowledge our sins to the Lord.

All: **Faithful God,**
I confess that your new law
has not permeated my heart.

You are my God
but I have not kept our covenant.

With the help of all your holy ones, living and dead,
renew in me
the presence of your Holy Spirit
so I can bring your reconciliation and hope
to all.

Litany of contrition

God reaches out to those who ask for forgiveness. Let us open ourselves to God's love.

God of mercy,	**Forgive us.**
God of faithfulness,	**Forgive us.**
Reconciling God,	**Forgive us.**
God who leads us back,	**Forgive us.**
God of the new covenant,	**Forgive us.**
God of unconditional love,	**Forgive us.**
God of the weak,	**Help us to care.**
God of the poor,	**Help us to care.**
God of the discounted,	**Help us to care.**
God of the abused,	**Help us to care.**
God of refugees and the homeless,	**Help us to care.**
God of the hungry,	**Help us to care.**
God of the victimized,	**Help us to care.**
God of the abandoned,	**Help us to care.**
God of understanding,	**Strengthen us.**
God of wisdom,	**Strengthen us.**
God of life,	**Strengthen us.**
Patient God,	**Strengthen us.**
God of justice,	**Strengthen us.**
God of hope,	**Strengthen us.**
God of peace,	**Strengthen us.**

We pray together the greatest prayer of forgiveness:

Our Father

(sung)

Silent prayer/reflection for conversion of heart

Proclamation of praise

Concluding prayer of thanksgiving

Loving God,
the forgiveness you lavish on us
through your son, Jesus,
has brought us back to life.

With praise and gratitude
we ask that your Holy Spirit
may etch the new covenant
on our hearts as never before.

Keep us aware
of your living presence
in us
and in all people.

Give us the grace of commitment
to live our new covenant
in spirit and in truth.

We ask this of you, Father, Son, and Holy Spirit.

All: Amen.

Conclusion

Blessing

May our gracious God bless, empower, and sustain us.

All: Amen.

Dismissal

Go with the security of God's love, and care for one another.

All: We will, with God's help!

Closing song

Resources

Keeping the Covenant—Lent, Cycle B

Scripture reflection suggestions for *Jer 31:31–34* and *Mk 12:28–34*

God's decision to establish a new covenant, as recorded by Jeremiah, is a call to the interior life, to live a life directed by the Spirit. There is no longer a place for legalism, for feeling good just because we have kept the rules. The heart of the new covenant is the spirit of love that directs our actions. The following ideas are offered at this Lenten time of conversion.

1. The scribe in Mark's gospel was "not far from the kingdom of God" (*Mk 12:34*) when he recognized that loving his neighbor was a much deeper living of the covenant than offering sacrifice and doing personal penance. Consider these ideas:

   - Who is my neighbor?

   - Do I experience God's love for me as a call to extend generous love to others?

   - Does my living of Lent focus on stockpiling acts of denial, or on becoming a more loving person through acts of service and experiences of prayer?

   - What needs of my neighbor can I try to support?

   - How and why do I ignore the needs of others?

   - To what "neighborhood" am I most able to extend care?

   - Do I see Lent as an opportunity for sacrifice, or for compassion and loving service as well?

2. "I will place my law within them, and write it upon their hearts; I will be their God, and they shall be my people" (*Jer 31:33*). According to Jeremiah, we all have a knowledge of God and the ways of God written on our collective heart. We are the community of God's people. This reading and this season provide an opportunity to reflect on conscience and its role personally and within the community.

   - What is conscience?

   - How is it formed?

   - What is this law placed within my heart?

   - How does the larger community help in conscience formation?

   - When conflicts in choosing arise in my life, how does conscience guide me?

   - How does conscience keep me faithful to my covenant?

3. Central to our life as God's people is the ministry of reconciliation. As we, the Church, are reconciled, we are being prepared to welcome others home. Loving our neighbor who is disconnected from the community through misunderstanding, inactivity, anger, and hurt is not only keeping the covenant, but helping to renew the covenant in the hearts and lives of all God's people. Perhaps the scripture reflection could focus on this dimension of outreach to others based on the assembly's desire to live its covenant more fully. The following are some reflection questions.

- How do I feel when I am reconciled with God and with others?

- Do I know anyone that lives without this experience of reconciliation?

- What are some ways that reconciliation, the renewal of the covenant, is available to them?

- What can I do to extend this reconciliation and renewal to them?

- What do I need to do to prepare myself to be a person of reconciliation?

Music suggestions

Opening and closing songs

"All My Days," by Dan Schutte, S.J. and Jim Murray, S.J.
(*Glory and Praise*)

"Grant To Us, O Lord," by Lucien Deiss, C.S.Sp.
(*People's Mass Book*)

"Remember Your Love," by Mike Balhoff, Darryl Ducote, and Gary Daigle (*Glory and Praise*)

"Sing Out His Goodness," by Darryl Ducote (*Glory and Praise*)

"For You Are My God," by John Foley, S.J. (*Glory and Praise*)

"Yahweh, the Faithful One," by Dan Schutte, S.J. (*Glory and Praise*)

Responsorial psalm

"Be With Me, Lord," by Marty Haugen (*Gather to Remember*)
(alternate suggestion to *Psalm 111* in printed service)

Gospel acclamation—a common melody

Song of contrition

"Pardon Your People," by Carey Landry (*Glory and Praise*)

Proclamation of Praise

"We Praise You," by Daryl Ducote and Gary Daigle (*Glory and Praise*)

"Song of Thanksgiving," by Darryl Ducote (*Glory and Praise*)

"Though the Mountains May Fall," by Dan Schutte, S.J.
(*Glory and Praise*)

Our Father—chant recommended; or a familiar sung version

Reflection music

The Fairy Ring by Mike Rowland (Antiquity Records)

Rain Dance by Philip Elcano (Desert Productions)

Environment suggestion

This penitential service presents our covenant relationship, expressed most concretely, through our love of neighbor. A simple suggestion for environment would be to place baskets at the entrance of the church for canned food and other nonperishable products. As the people arrive, they can place their contributions in the baskets. These items can be given to the local food pantry or parish social service group for distribution at any time. A simple, unpretentious placing of the baskets before the assembly, as the service is about to begin, is all that needs to be done. The gift of food will speak for itself.

Further suggestions

1. *Psalm 111*, the *responsorial*, can be prayed in choirs if desired.

2. The *Responsorial Psalm* and the *Litany of Contrition* have alternate musical suggestions in the music resource section. If these alternatives are used do not print *Psalm 111* and/or the *Litany of Contrition* in the service for the assembly.

3. The *Litany of Contrition* can be led by a lector or a penitent in the assembly. It could be prayed in choirs, or in sections, or in alternating voices. If you try a new way for the assembly to participate in prayer together, choose strong voices and give clear directions in advance.

4. For suggestions on how to *present* the *examination of conscience*, see the Advent reconciliation services.

5. Reflection music during the time of *silent prayer/reflection for conversion of heart* supports personal prayer. If music ministers are not able to provide live, meditative music, the suggestions given in the *music resource section* may be helpful.

Becoming a New Creation

Gathering

Opening song

Greeting

> May God's transforming love touch your mind and heart.

Response: And yours as well!

Introduction

> The choices of our heart are what make us holy. In Scripture, the heart is the vital center of human life. Our thoughts, our plans, our understanding comes from the heart. If these movements of the heart are evil, our heart loses its ability to love and turns to stone. The salvation God offers is the chance for us to be radically transformed. God offers a new heart, one that will be changed at the core, one of flesh, one making us a new person, saturated with the Holy Spirit.
>
> Let us look into our hearts now and examine our need for God's saving forgiveness.

Opening prayer

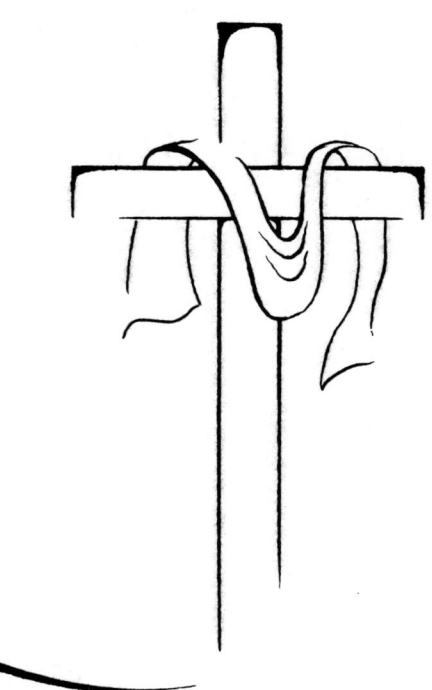

> Persistent God,
> who gathers us,
> whose love for us is unconditional,
> we come asking to be changed.
>
> Our hearts are hard.
>
> As much as we try
> we do not love as we ought.
>
> Change our stony hearts.
>
> Give us new hearts
> to reflect your generous and wise love.
>
> We want to become the persons
> you call us to be.
>
> We ask this in Jesus' name.

Response: Amen.

Celebration of the Word of God

First reading: *Ez 36:24–28*

Responsorial psalm: *Ps 51:3–21*

> **Response: Have mercy on me, O God, in your goodness.**
>
>> Have mercy on me, O God, in your goodness;
>>> in the greatness of your compassion wipe out my offense.
>> Thoroughly wash me from my guilt
>>> and of my sin cleanse me.

Response

>> For I acknowledge my offense,
>>> and my sin is before me always:
>> "Against you only have I sinned,
>>> and done what is evil in your sight"—
>> That you may be justified in your sentence,
>>> vindicated when you condemn.
>> Indeed, in guilt was I born,
>>> and in sin my mother conceived me;

Response

>> Behold, you are pleased with sincerity of heart,
>>> and in my inmost being you teach me wisdom.
>> Cleanse me of sin with hyssop, that I may be purified;
>>> wash me, and I shall be whiter than snow.
>> Let me hear the sounds of joy and gladness;
>>> the bones you have crushed shall rejoice.
>> Turn away your face from my sins,
>>> and blot out all my guilt.

Response

>> A clean heart create for me, O God,
>>> and a steadfast spirit renew within me.
>> Cast me not out from your presence,
>>> and your holy spirit take not from me.
>> Give me back the joy of your salvation,
>>> and a willing spirit sustain in me.
>> I will teach transgressors your ways,
>>> and sinners shall return to you.

Response

>> Free me from blood guilt, O God, my saving God;
>>> then my tongue shall revel in your justice.
>> O Lord, open my lips,
>>> and my mouth shall proclaim your praise.
>> For you are not pleased with sacrifices;
>>> should I offer a holocaust, you would not accept it.
>> My sacrifice, O God, is a contrite spirit;
>>> a heart contrite and humbled, O God, you will not spurn.

Response

> Be bountiful, O LORD, to Zion in your
>   kindness
>   by rebuilding the walls of Jerusalem;
> Then shall you be pleased with due
>   sacrifices,
>   burnt offerings and holocausts;
>   then shall they offer up bullocks on
>   your altar.

Response

Second reading: *2 Cor 5:17–21*

(period of silence)

Gospel acclamation

Glory and praise to you, Lord Jesus Christ!

> Teach us to number our days aright,
> that we may gain wisdom of heart. (*Ps 90:12*)

Glory and praise to you, Lord Jesus Christ!

Gospel: *Lk 22:31–34*

Scripture reflection

Examination of conscience

Let us kneel and look into our hearts, often turned hard as stone, to find what keeps us from loving as God's grace empowers us to do.

- What or who has taken the first place in my heart?
- If God is not at the center of my values and choices, why not?
- How have I denied God, given lip service, like Peter, but not a commitment of the heart?
- In what ways have I nurtured God's place in my heart?

- Am I growing in self appreciation while also recognizing that my positive qualities come from God?
- What about myself do I thank God for?
- What about myself gets out of control?
- Do I ever take things out on others because I am upset with myself?
- What do I need to soften this hardness in myself?

- As Christ's ambassador, do I bring his reconciliation to my daily living?
- How do I exercise responsible loving toward my family?

- Against what family need have I hardened my heart? With whom should I talk to resolve this?

- How do I respond at work when Jesus' values of integrity and respect for all are challenged?

- In what ways and with whom do I model justice and compassion? How consistent am I in this behavior?

- How am I working to allow God's Spirit to take hold of my heart and make me God's new creation?

Celebration of Reconciliation

Our hearts are open. Let us acknowledge our sins before the Lord.

All: **I confess to you, loving God,**
and to my sisters and brothers,
my faith family here present,
that I have sinned through my own fault.

My thoughts, words, and deeds,
my failures to fulfill my baptismal call to love and to reconcile,
all witness to my sins.

I ask for the prayers
of everyone who knows God,
the angels, our mother, Mary, the saints, especially Peter,
and all people living and dead.

I ask particularly that everyone here present
pray for me to the Lord our God.

God is merciful and very loving. God renews our hearts through the abundance of the Holy Spirit. Let us ask for hearts of flesh to lead us into the days ahead.

Song of contrition

Lord's Prayer

Together let us pray the prayer that will lead us to conversion of heart.

All: **Our Father, who art in heaven, . . .**

Merciful God,
like Peter, we know our weaknesses
and long to be forgiven.
Make our hearts one with you again.
We ask this in Jesus' name.

All: **Amen.**

Silent prayer/reflection for conversion of heart

Proclamation of praise for God's mercy: *Ps 34:2, 4–9, 12–19, 22–23*

God has gathered us, given us a new heart, and placed the love of the Holy Spirit deeply within us once again. Let us praise God!

Response: **I will bless the Lord at all times;**
his praise shall be ever in my mouth.

Glorify the LORD with me,
let us together extol his name.
I sought the LORD, and he answered me
and delivered me from all my fears.

Response

Look to him that you may be radiant with joy,
and your faces may not blush with shame.
When the afflicted man called out, the LORD heard,
and from all his distress he saved him.
The angel of the LORD encamps
around those who fear him, and delivers them.
Taste and see how good the Lord is;
happy the man who takes refuge in him.

Response

Come, children, hear me;
I will teach you the fear of the LORD.
Which of you desires life,
and takes delight in prosperous days?
Keep your tongue from evil
and your lips from speaking guile;
Turn from evil, and do good;
seek peace, and follow after it.

Response

The LORD has eyes for the just,
and ears for their cry.
The LORD confronts the evildoers,
to destroy remembrance of them from the earth.
When the just cry out, the LORD hears them,
and from all their distress he rescues them.
The LORD is close to the brokenhearted;
and those who are crushed in spirit he saves.

Response

Vice slays the wicked,
and the enemies of the just pay for
their guilt.
But the LORD redeems the lives of his
servants;
no one incurs guilt who takes refuge
in him.

Response

Concluding prayer of thanksgiving

Loving God,
you change our hearts.

We experience again your promise to be our God.

We are your new creation
through the forgiveness of the Holy Spirit.

May this reconciliation help us to be ambassadors for Jesus.

May we, like Peter, strengthen our sisters and brothers
as we walk the journey of conversion together.

We ask this in Jesus' name.

All: **Amen.**

Sign of peace

Now, with hearts renewed, let us exchange a sign of peace and joy.

Conclusion

Blessing

May God, whose fidelity transforms our hearts, strengthen us!

All: **Amen.**

May Jesus, whose love makes us a new creation, guide us!

All: **Amen.**

May the Holy Spirit, whose presence is our joy, bless us!

All: **Amen.**

Dismissal

Go in peace to reconcile and renew our sisters and brothers.

All: **We will, with joyful hearts!**

Closing song

Resources

Becoming a New Creation—Lent, Cycle C

Scripture reflection suggestions for *Ez 36:24–28, 2 Cor 5:17–21* and *Lk 22:31–34*

1. "Have you been saved?" is a question frequently asked by our fundamentalist sisters and brothers. It can be threatening to Catholics because we understand salvation as a process that extends over a lifetime. Paul tells us clearly (*2 Cor 5:17*) that we are a new creation. Not only are we saved, but God lovingly and consistently continues to walk with us on our journey of life. Some reflection questions to guide the *scripture reflection* around the idea of salvation as a process are as follows.

   - How do life experiences reveal to us that salvation is a process of commitments and failures?

   - What part does God play and what part do we play in this process?

   - How do we measure the quality of our commitment?

   - Why is it that Peter's denial does not condemn him?

   - Why is it that God continues to gather us and reconcile us generation after generation?

   - When is the process of conversion completed in us?

2. Paul tells us that we are ambassadors for Christ (*2 Cor 5:20*). We know, however, that we do not always fulfill our call. Jesus tells Peter, "and once you have turned back, you must strengthen your brothers" (*Lk 22:32*). Our failures and sins can make us supportive companions on the journey of salvation. Reflecting on this role, born out of our weakness, can be the subject of a *scripture reflection*. The following are suggested reflection questions.

   - Why does Paul call us ambassadors for Christ?

   - How seriously do I take my role as Christ's ambassador?

   - Is the working out of salvation primarily between God and me, or are others a significant part of the process?

   - How can sin make us wiser and more compassionate?

   - How do we become healers?

   - Is there any significance to Peter being chosen as the leader of the infant church?

3. Evil is clearly present in our world. The evil spirit approaches every-one. Selfishness, possessiveness, prejudice, control, anger, laziness, and pride can seem to be virtues when the spirit of evil presents them to our stony hearts. Jesus tells Peter and us,"Simon, Simon, behold Satan has demanded to sift all of you like wheat, but I have prayed that your own faith may not fail" (*Lk 22:31–32*). The following reflection questions can be used.

- How do I know what is evil?
- Why is evil often subtle?
- If I am in a situation in which I sense evil, what do I do?
- How does evil take control of my heart?
- What does it mean to hate sin but love the sinner?
- How can I find help in avoiding evil?

Music suggestions

Opening and closing songs

"Hosea," by Gregory Norbet, O.S.B. (*Glory and Praise*)

"Deep Within," by David Haas (*Who Calls You By Name*, Vol. I, G.I.A. Publications)

"Change Our Hearts," by Rory Cooney (*Glory and Praise*)

"You Are Near," by Dan Schutte, S.J. (*Glory and Praise*)

Responsorial psalm

"Create in Me a Clean Heart," by David Haas (*Who Calls You By Name*, Vol. I, G.I.A. Publications) (alternate suggestion to *Psalm 51* in printed service)

Song of contrition

"Change Our Hearts," by Rory Cooney (*Glory and Praise*)

"Grant to Us, O Lord," by Lucian Deiss, C.S.Sp. (*People's Mass Book*)

Reflection Music

On Wings of Peace by Danny Bouchard (Daughters of St. Paul)

Solace by Mike Rowland (Antiquity Records)

Environment suggestion

Lent has but one focus—conversion of heart, a change of life patterns. The Scripture, in delivering that message, leads us to prayer. In prayerfully hearing the word of God, we experience its power to convert us. That power is the presence of the Holy Spirit entering our hearts.

Since each person brings a heart to this penitential service, consider that to be the environment in which the celebration takes place. Many hearts joined in prayer and reconciliation create and shape the heart of the community that is present. No external ritual or setting can convey the deeply known experience of conversion of heart. In sharing the sign of peace before the last blessing we celebrate our conversion.

So, let the Scripture do its work, and let the hearts of all present be the real environment in which we experience conversion. The joy of that conversion will be in striking contrast to the usual, appropriate, purple cloth, and simple cross. Let the contrast acknowledge that sin is always a part of our lives, but reconciliation is always a part of our journey, as well. We are always both!

Further suggestions

1. The *Responsorial psalm, Ps 51*, can be recited by alternating verses within the assembly, side to side, or section by section, with everyone praying the response. If the alternate song response, "Create in Me a Clean Heart" is used, *Ps 51* can be eliminated from the copies made for the assembly.

2. If *Ps 51* (the Responsorial printed in the service) is used, singing the *gospel acclamation* would provide variation for prayer. Use a simple melody (one known by the assembly) for the acclamation and a simple chant for the verse. In the same vein, if a song is substituted for the *Responsorial psalm*, reciting the *gospel acclamation* will provide variation.

3. The Advent reconciliation services provide ideas to *present* the *examination of conscience*. In any case, having members of the assembly lead this particular one may be most effective. Since it is not lengthy, silent pauses between sections, or even between individual questions, can provide participants with reflection time.

4. The suggestion offered to pray *Ps 51*, the *Responsorial Psalm*, can be effective for the *proclamation of praise, Ps 34*, especially if the assembly has experienced this manner of prayer earlier in the service. (See number 1 above.)

5. To provide time for personal prayer, *reflection music* is encouraged during the time of *silent prayer/reflection for conversion of heart*. Music ministers often enjoy playing simple, prayerful music. It has the power to center us. If live music is not possible, the music suggestion section offers tapes or compact discs.

At Times of Renewal, Recommitment, New Beginnings

Living in the Spirit

Gathering

Opening reflection music

(extended listening)

Prayer

(stand)

Let us pray.

Freeing God
we come before you
weighed down by our sins.

Open us to your Holy Spirit.

Guide us back to your love.

We want to live again
in the freedom that is ours
as your own people.

We ask this through Jesus Christ, our Lord.

All: **Amen.**

Joy   Generosity   Patience

Faithfulness

Peace   Love   Self-control

Gentleness   Kindness

Celebration of the Word of God

Reading: *Gal 5:13–15, 18–25*

> *(extended silence)*

Responsorial psalm: *130:1–8*

> **Response:** **Out of the depths I cry to you, O Lord;**
> **Lord, hear my voice!**
>
> Out of the depths I cry to you, O
> > Lord;
> > Lord, hear my voice!
> Let your ears be attentive
> > to my voice in supplication:
>
> **Response**
>
> If you, O Lord, mark iniquities,
> > Lord, who can stand?
> But with you is forgiveness,
> > that you may be revered.
>
> **Response**
>
> I trust in the Lord;
> > my soul trust in his word.
> My soul waits for the Lord
> > more than sentinels wait for the
> > > dawn.
>
> **Response**
>
> More than sentinels wait for the dawn,
> > let Israel wait for the Lord,
> For with the Lord is kindness
> > and with him is plenteous redemption;
> And he will redeem Israel
> > from all their iniquities.
>
> **Response**

Scripture reflection

> *(period of silence)*

Prayers of intercession

> Let us ask the Holy Spirit to free us.
> *(kneel)*

Leader:	That we may know our sins,	**Come, Holy Spirit.**
	That we will reject the works of the flesh,	**Come, Holy Spirit.**
	That God will move among us with forgiveness,	**Come, Holy Spirit.**
	That we will forgive one another,	**Come, Holy Spirit.**

That we may use our freedom
    to serve one another,   **Come, Holy Spirit.**
That we live beyond the
    directives of the law,   **Come, Holy Spirit.**
That we may belong to Jesus Christ, **Come, Holy Spirit.**
That we will be committed to
    building the kingdom of God,   **Come, Holy Spirit.**

Song of intercession

Celebration of Reconciliation

All: **I confess to you,**
        redeeming God,
        and to all your chosen people,
        especially those here present,
        that I have sinned
        in thought, word, and deed.

        I have refused to live by your Spirit.
        I ask the prayers of your holy ones in heaven,
        and my sisters and brothers here,
        to help me reject evil and its attractions,
        and live in the grace and power of your Holy Spirit.

Lord's Prayer

(stand)

Sign of peace

Let us encourage one another and witness
to the power of the Holy Spirit among us
by offering a sign of peace.

Conclusion

Reflection music

(continued extended listening)

Resources

Living in the Spirit

Scripture reflection suggestions for *Gal 5:13–15, 18–25*

1. We can miss the power of the grace of reconciliation if we get caught up in being contrite simply for individual acts that weaken and/or endanger our relationship with God, others, and ourselves. The reading from Galatians lists sinful acts, but Paul's theology of sin goes beyond listing and apologizing for specific acts. Walter Burghardt, S.J., in *Towards Reconciliation*, distinguishes between sin and sins after citing Paul's experience of being unable to do the good he willed (*Rom 7:19*). Reconciliation for Paul means conversion and so we look at individual sins only to see what sort of person these sins express. Probing the sin in our lives, not the sins, is the basis of reconciliation. The following are suggested reflection questions.

   - Why do I do the sinful things I do?

   - Is there a repetitious pattern in the sinful acts I commit?

   - Is there a common root for my sinful acts?

   - What tendencies in me pull me into sinful acts?

   - Have I grown into being a more caring, just, self-sacrificing person? If not, why not?

   - What would I have to change in me so Jesus could freely do the work of conversion?

2. Paul is clear that we do not live by the law (*Gal 5:18*). We are free of those strictures. Our choices are governed by a much broader vision, namely love. The demands of love, love of God and love of neighbor, are the guidelines by which we judge ourselves as followers of Jesus. The depth of our commitment to Jesus can be realized by comparing the ten commandments to Jesus' law of love or by comparing the ten commandments to the Beatitudes. The Spirit guides us in living these demands of love. Reflect on this comparison.

3. To prayerfully think about the growth of the fruits of the Holy Spirit within us is motivating and energizing. A *Scripture reflection* could present these powers of the Holy Spirit (They are listed on the printed service). Assist the assembly to select one which is appropriate for individual consideration. The following are suggestions to guide the reflection on an individual fruit of the Holy Spirit:

   • Which fruit of the Holy Spirit is an antidote to my root sin?

   • What in my life needs to change for this power of the Holy Spirit to grow?

   • What steps might I take to begin that change?

   Give reflection time between the questions. At the conclusion of this time, suggest that each person formulate a prayer (even write it on their printed service in an empty space) asking the Holy Spirit to deepen that fruit in his or her life. Give sufficient time for the assembly to shape the prayers.

   Conclude by affirming the tremendous power of the Holy Spirit, and then begin to pray the *prayers of intercession*.

Music suggestions

Reflection music

> "Veni Creator," by Danny Bouchard (*On Wings of Peace*, Daughters of St. Paul)

> "Veni Sancte Spiritus," by Jacques Berthier (*Songs and Prayers from Taize*, G.I.A. Publications, Inc.)

Song of intercession

> "Spirit of the Living God," by Dan Iverson (EMI Christian Music) (Sing as many times as needed.)

> "Send Us Your Spirit," by David Haas (*Music Issue 1995*, #554)

> "Lord, Send Out Your Spirit," by Mike Balhoff, Gary Daigle, and Darryl Ducote (*Glory and Praise*, verses 2, 4, 5)

Lord's Prayer

> Use a simple chant or a familiar melody.

Environment suggestions

The primary symbol in this reconciliation service is the Word of God, bringing alive the power of the Holy Spirit among us. Place the Scriptures simply and beautifully before the assembly. Choose a stand that is well made, of authentic material and display the Scripture book so all can see it easily.

You may want to consider seating the assembled community in a circle or semi-circle, if this will facilitate common prayer. If that is the arrangement, the Scripture can be placed in the center of the circle or at the open end.

Since water is a symbol of the Holy Spirit as well, some lush, green plants, signaling vibrant life, can be placed with the Scripture. If the enthroned Bible is to be used for the reading, make sure it can be reached easily by the lector and taken to the place of proclamation.

Consider this variation of the preceding idea:

Fire is also a symbol of the Holy Spirit, as is the color red. If it is a fitting liturgical time, consider the use of red cloth to enhance the Scripture stand, perhaps as a hanging panel. The Bible itself can have a red cover. Remind the assembly of the living nature of the Scriptures by placing a red candle, or candles, near it. Using red glass votive containers in which you can burn white candles makes it easy to have red candle lights. Do not multiply candles or other supporting symbols. Simplicity is always the key to a prayerful environment. Too much distracts.

Further suggestions

1. The *gathering time* for this service with a lay leader of prayer begins gently. The *reflection music* can begin several minutes before the established time of the service, so as people enter the worship space, a prayerful atmosphere is already in place.

2. The lay leader of prayer can be seated with the assembly at the beginning of the service and move to the leader's place for the opening of prayer.

3. The *responsorial Psalm* can be led by a lector, or the assembly can pray it in choirs, with the response said by everyone.

4. The *prayers of intercession* can be led by the lay leader, a lector, or individuals from the assembly (with enough volume). Balance and participation in community prayer are two factors that make communal prayer meaningful and rich.

Being Lost, Being Found

Gathering

Opening reflection music

> *(extended listening)*

Prayer

> *(stand)*
>
> Let us pray.
>
> Searching God,
> we come before you, lost,
> and in need of being found.
>
> We have examined our hearts
> for signs of your presence,
> but find distraction and darkness.
>
> Open us to your reconciling love.
>
> Bring us back to you
> for the joy of your people,
> for the integrity of our hearts,
> and for the praise of your glorious name.
>
> We ask this through Jesus, our Lord.

All: **Amen.**

Celebration of the Word of God

Reading: *Jer 29:11–13*

    (period of silence)

Responsorial psalm: *Psalm 139:1–18, 23–24*

    Response: O Lord, you have probed me and you know me.

        O Lord, you have probed me and you know me;
          you know when I sit and when I stand;
          you understand my thoughts from afar.
        My journeys and my rest you scrutinize,
          with all my ways you are familiar.
        Even before a word is on my tongue,
          behold, O Lord, you know the whole of it.
        Behind me and before, you hem me in
          and rest your hand upon me.
        Such knowledge is too wonderful for me;
          too lofty for me to attain.

Response

        Where can I go from your spirit?
          from your presence where can I flee?
        If I go up to the heavens, you are there;
          if I sink to the nether world, you are present there.
        If I take the wings of the dawn,
          if I settle at the farthest limits of the sea,
         Even there your hand shall guide me,
          and your right hand hold me fast.
        If I say, "Surely the darkness shall hide me,
          and night shall be my light"—
        For you darkness itself is not dark,
          and night shines as the day.
          [Darkness and light are the same.]

Response

        Truly you have formed my inmost being;
          you knit me in my mother's womb.
        I give you thanks that I am fearfully,
          wonderfully made;
          wonderful are your works.
        My soul also you knew full well;
          nor was my frame unknown to you
        When I was made in secret,
          when I was fashioned in the depths
            of the earth.

Your eyes have seen my actions;
in your book they are all written;
my days were limited before one of them existed.
How weighty are your designs, O God;
how vast the sum of them!
Were I to recount them, they would
outnumber the sands;
did I reach the end of them, I should
still be with you.

Response

Probe me, O God, and know my heart;
try me, and know my thoughts;
See if my way is crooked,
and lead me in the way of old.

Response

Second Reading: *1 Jn 5:13–15*

(period of silence)

Gospel acclamation: *Jn 15:7*

Alleluia *(sung)*

If you abide in me, and my words
abide in you, ask for whatever you
wish, and it will be done for you.

Alleluia

Gospel: *Lk 15:1–3, 8–10*

Scripture Reflection

(period of silence)

Prayers of intercession

(kneel)

Response: O Lord, Hear My Prayer *(sung)*

That we will search for the Lord with renewed purpose,
That we will trust in the ways of the Lord,
That we will confidently place our future in the Lord's care,

Response

That we will look for the Lord in each circumstance of our life,
That we will live believing God hears our request,
That we will commit ourselves to prayer,

Response

That we will honestly admit our sin,
That we accept God's constant and unconditional love,
That we will value our body temple, gift of the Lord,

Response

That we will search out the rejected and sorrowing,
That we will sweep our world of injustice and violence,
That we will light our homes with love and peace.

Response

That we will rejoice in the lost being found,
That we will call others together in unity,
That we will repent of our refusal to respond more deeply to
God's call,

Response

Song of intercession

Celebration of Reconciliation

All: **I confess to you,
saving God,
to all of the angels and saints,
and to everyone here present
that I have sinned.**

                **I've lost my way to you
through selfish and irresponsible choices.**

                **I ask the support of all the holy ones who stand in your presence,
and the prayers of everyone here.**

Lord's prayer

(stand)

Sign of peace

Our acceptance of one another is a sign
that we have been found by God.

Let us show God's saving love with a sign of peace.

Conclusion

Reflection music

(continued extended listening)

Resources
Being Lost, Being Found

Scripture reflection suggestions for *Jer 29:11–13; 1 Jn 5:14–15; and Lk 15:1–3, 8–10*

1. We find it hard to believe that God comes looking for us when our relationships become weak. We seem to believe that we go looking for God. When discomfort sets in, we think we take the initiative to return to God. That isn't how the parable in Luke presents the situation. The woman, an image for God, does all the searching and then holds a celebration. What material for reflection! The following questions may help you to begin.

   - Does my image of God agree with the vitally concerned, caring, outgoing, even feminine, picture of God presented in the Scripture? How is it different? Why?
   - What feelings do I have when I think of God as eager to find the lost one?
   - How would I describe my relationship with God?
   - Is God asking any change of me in how I relate to God? How do I need to respond to God?

2. In *1 Jn 5:14* we hear a reference to God's will. God's will is clear if we must choose between good and evil. However, for many people choices can be between two goods or involve two situations in which the outcome cannot be known with certainty. What is God's will here? Reflecting on how to find and follow God's will may provide an opportunity for adult spiritual development. Consider these initial questions:

   - Is this a choice between good and evil?
   - What role does my experience and common sense play in identifying God's will?
   - How does my choice affect my present responsibilities?
   - Does following God's will mean there is only one way to respond?
   - What role does my faith community have in my decision?
   - What is the presence of the Holy Spirit within me saying?
   - What would Jesus do?

Music suggestions

Opening/closing reflection music

> "O Lord, Hear My Prayer," by Jacques Berthier (*Taizé—Wait for the Lord*, G.I.A. Publications)

Responsorial psalm

> "You've Searched Me," by David Haas (*As Water to the Thirsty*, G.I.A. Publications)
> (alternate to *Psalm 139* printed in service)

Gospel acclamation—Choose a prayerful alleluia familiar to your assembly.

Song of intercession

> "Amazing Grace," (*Music Issue 1995*, #406)
> "This Alone," by Tim Manion (*Glory and Praise*)

Environment suggestion

The readings tell of God's future hope-filled plans for us. God is listening to our cries. We are lost, but being found as the woman lights her lamp and searches relentlessly. We are the lost coin, a valuable treasure in God's eyes.

Place the Scriptures simply and beautifully in the presence of the assembly. If the liturgical season permits, use the color white or silver. Drape the Scripture stand in fabric or use the fabric in whatever way adds grace, beauty, and fluid lines to the setting. A subtle, but appropriate, addition would be a large vase filled with the dry plant called the money tree or honesty plant (the botanical name is "lunaria"). Its silver oviates resemble coins. If this is not available, white seasonal flowers will add vitality.

Shine strong, focused light on the Scripture, or use white candles or a large white or clear votive light to recall God's determined searching presence.

Further suggestions

1. The opening *reflection music* by Taizé can begin a few minutes early so as to have a prayerful, reflective atmosphere established as the assembly arrives. The music should continue for a good while to help people center.

2. The opening *reflection music* by Taizé can be sung by the music ministers, or you may want to simply play the music tape or compact disc (5½ minutes). Either way, hearing the repetitious refrain will then make it easy for the assembly to sing it as a response to the *prayers of intercession*.

3. The alternate sung *responsorial psalm* by David Haas might be more challenging for the assembly to sing. If done by musicians, it is beautifully meditative. Do not include *Psalm 139* in the assembly copy if you choose this alternate.

4. See the music suggestions for a *gospel acclamation*.

5. *Prayers of intercession*—since the intercessions are in groups of three, use three different voices in the same sequence to prayerfully read aloud each group. Have the assembly sing the response after each triad. The assembly will know the response since it was used as centering music at the opening of this service.

6. The service closes with a return to the opening *reflection music*. Persons who want to continue to pray and reflect can do so. It also allows those who are ready to leave to do so in a meditative spirit.

Forgiving in Love

(Communal Celebration for Couples)

Gathering

Opening reflection music

(extended listening)

Prayer

(stand)

Let us pray.

God,
you have told us you are love,
and when we love each other,
it is your very presence we experience.

We are sometimes weak in our love.

Give us open, forgiving hearts
to renew our mutual commitment to each other
and to be a sign of your life
for all.

We ask this in Jesus' name.

All: **Amen.**

Celebration of the Word of God

Reading: *Col 3:12–17*

(period of silence)

Responsorial psalm: *Psalm 145:8–10, 15, 17–18*

Response: **The LORD is gracious and merciful,**
slow to anger and of great kindness.

The LORD is gracious and merciful,
slow to anger and of great kindness.
The LORD is good to all
and compassionate toward all his works.

Response

Let all your works give you thanks, O LORD,
and let your faithful ones bless you.
The eyes of all look hopefully to you,
and you give them their food in
due season;

Response

The LORD is just in all his ways
and holy in all his works.
The LORD is near to all who call upon him,
to all who call upon him in truth.

Response

(period of silence)

Scripture reflection

Examination of conscience

Before your conversation as a couple, take some time to reflect privately. The following questions are meant only to facilitate honest, meaningful conversation with your spouse. Consider them, or your own circumstances, before you express to each other your concerns about your marriage. What must each do to renew and strengthen your life together?

- What concerns me most about our relationship? How do I handle that concern? What is not going well? What do I need to do to improve our dealing with this circumstance?

- What gives me energy, motivation, peace, and trust in our relationship? How do I express that to my spouse? Are there ways I take our relationship for granted?

- What in our family life is weak? Does someone or something need to be challenged? How can I contribute to make this situation healthier and more life-giving?

- What place does God hold in our home? Does my example lead us closer to the Lord or take us away?

- What will be my main commitment at this time to renew and strengthen our marriage?

Celebration of Reconciliation

General conversation

When couples are ready to talk about their life together, they should go to a place of relative privacy.

Prayer of Sorrow

As couples complete their sharing, a prayer of sorrow can be prayed together, either as individuals or as a couple. If needed, a suggested prayer follows, but spontaneous prayers are very appropriate.

Loving and merciful God,
I am sorry for the ways
I have refused to love my wife/husband, _____.
I ask her/his forgiveness, too.   *(name)*

I want to be your loving presence
for my whole family.

Give me what I need, especially gentleness and patience.

I intend to open my heart more completely
to your guidance.

Touch my days
with praise and gratitude to you,
who have been so compassionate to me.

Amen.

Prayers of intercession

Wives and husbands may now want to pray for their own needs, the needs of family, or other concerns they have as disciples of Jesus. As one offers a petition, the other may want to respond, "Hear us, Lord," or in whatever way is comfortable.

As couples are ready, they return to the larger group.

Song of recommitment

Lord's Prayer

(Stand)

Let us pray together Jesus's words of petition, love, and commitment.

Our Father . . .

Sign of peace

Peace is the fruit of love. Let us share this sign with each other and those around us.

Conclusion

Closing song

Resources
Communal Celebration for Couples

Suggestions for Scripture Reflection for *Col 3:12–17* and *Ps 145, 8–10, 15 and 17–18.*

Both Scripture passages present the life-giving characteristics of love. We experience them when God is loving us and when we are loving one another. These experiences can be and often are indelible ones. To dwell a few minutes on people's understanding of these experiences or emptiness when they are absent may be sufficient groundwork to prepare each couple to share in the upcoming moments. It seems important to place a priority on their time of mutual conversation rather than on the Scripture reflection time.

Music suggestions

Opening reflection music

> "Ubi Caritas," by Jacques Berthier *(Taizé—Cantate!*, G.I.A. Publications)

> "Live in Charity," (Ubi Caritas) by Jacques Berthier (*Songs and Prayers from Taizé*, #49, G.I.A. Publications, Inc.)

Closing song

> "All My Days," by Dan Schutte (*Glory and Praise*)

> "Where Charity and Love Prevail," by Omer Westendorf and Paul Benoir, O.S.B. (*Rejoice*, #291)

> "We Have Been Told," by David Haas (*Glory and Praise*)

> "We Praise You," by Mike Balhoff, Daryl Ducote and Gary Daigle (*Glory and Praise*)

> "Yahweh, The Faithful One," by Dan Schutte (*Glory and Praise*)

Song of recommitment

> "Flower of Life," by Rufino Zaragoza, O.S.F. (*Light of Christ*, Oregon Catholic Press Publications)

> "St. Theresa's Prayer," by John Michael Talbot (*Heart of the Shepherd*, The Sparrow Corporation)

> "Dwelling Place," by John Foley, S.J. (*Glory and Praise*)

> "For You Are My God," by John Foley, S.J. (*Glory and Praise*)

> "Service," by Buddy Ceaser (*Glory and Praise*)

> "City of God," by Dan Schutte (*Glory and Praise*)

> "Hosea," by Gregory Norbet, O.S.B. (*Music Issue 1995*)

Environment suggestions

The Scripture is once again the environment in which we place ourselves. God's word directs our lives to the fidelity, trust, and self-sacrifice we need for keeping and developing our committed love.

Place the Bible before the group. Call attention to its presence with the color red. Fabric can do this with a hanging, or a stand cover, or a cascading piece in which gentle folds encompass not only the Bible itself, but perhaps some flowers or plant placed nearby. Arrange the Bible so it is easily accessible for the proclamation of the word. Lighting directed on the location of the Scripture also helps to focus on God's word. Red is traditionally the color of love, flowers and plants evidence of fruition, and light a symbol for the truth and goodness of the Lord. Whatever elements are used should be real and authentic. Simplicity and beauty are guidelines for an effective prayer environment.

Further suggestions

1. Consider dimming the lights when the time for individual *examination of conscience* begins. Keep them this way until the couples begin to return while the *song of recommitment* is played softly.

2. The *song of recommitment* can be played softly at first, but continuously, while the couples are coming back to the larger group. They may be encouraged to sing meditatively along until all have returned. Gradually the music can become fuller.

3. Because of the more personal interaction in this reconciliation service, consider holding a small celebration at the conclusion. The couples present and the circumstances in which the service is used will help you decide.

Forgiving in Love

(Celebration for Individual Couples)

Opening: Reflection music from resources following this celebration

Prayer

> Let us pray.
>
> God,
> you have told us you are love,
> and when we love each other,
> it is your very presence we experience.
>
> We are sometimes weak in our love.
>
> Give us open, forgiving hearts
> to renew our mutual commitment to each other
> and to be a sign of your life
> for all.
>
> We ask this in Jesus' name.

All: **Amen.**

Reading   from resources following this celebration, or personal choice
(period of silence)

Examination of conscience

Before your conversation as a couple, take some time to reflect privately. The following questions are meant only to facilitate honest, meaningful conversation with your spouse. Consider them, or your own circumstances, before you express to each other your concerns about your marriage. What must each do to renew and strengthen your life together?

- Are we as much in love now as when we first married?
- Am I?
- If not, is it my fault?
- Have I been faithful, have I trusted, have I believed?
- Have we grown careless, taking each other for granted?
- Am I too involved with my work?
- Am I interested enough in his work? In her work?
- Is our relationship with in-laws a thorny issue?
- Do we communicate very well?
- Do we easily share our inner feelings, both when we are happy and when we are hurt, when we are upset, and when we are content?
- Are family finances a sore spot?
- Do disagreements become arguments, then battles, then wars?
- Do we, at those times, often shout or swear or say vicious things?
- Have we been willing to forgive? Have I?
- Do we always make up before going to bed?
- Has our sexual life been satisfying? If not, have we discussed it honestly and tried to improve?
- Are we too self-centered as a family, not concerned enough about other families, about the Church, about the community in which we live?
- Do we get away now and then, just the two of us?
- Have we been good parents, loving, firm, understanding? Have I? Have we shared these responsibilities together?
- Has God slipped from our home?
- Does the example we give lead our children to the Lord or take them away from their Maker?
- Have we become selfish? Have I?
- Am I, are we, willing to begin again, to try harder, to give more?

General conversation

When you are ready, begin to talk about your life together.

Prayer of sorrow

When you complete your sharing, pray a prayer of sorrow together, either individually or as a couple. If needed, a suggested prayer follows, but spontaneous prayers are very appropriate.

Loving and merciful God,
I am sorry for the ways
I have refused to love my wife/husband, _____
I ask her/his forgiveness, too.   (name)
I want to be your loving presence
for my whole family.
Give me what I need, especially gentleness and patience.
I intend to open my heart more completely
to your guidance.
Touch my days
with praise and gratitude to you,
who have been so compassionate to me.

Amen.

Prayer of intercession

You may now want to pray for your own needs, the needs of family, or other concerns you have as disciples of Jesus. As one offers a petition, the other may want to respond, "Hear us, Lord," or in whatever way is comfortable.

Lord's Prayer

Sign of Peace

Closing

Your own personal celebration

Resources

Reflection music

> *True to the Journey*—especially side A—by Patrick Loomis
> (Candleflame Productions, Oregon Catholic Press Publications)
>
> *Comfort Zone* by Steven Halpern (Halpern Sounds,
> Credence Cassettes, Sheed and Ward Publications)
>
> *A New Dawn*—especially side B—by Katherine Chrishon
> (Candleflame Productions, Oregon Catholic Press Publications)
>
> Music of personal choice is most appropriate.

Scripture Readings

Hebrew Scriptures

> *Tobit 8:4–9*
>
> *Song of Songs 2:8–10, 14, 16a; 8:6–7a*

Christian Scriptures

> *1 Cor 12:14–26*
>
> *1 Cor 12:31–13:8a*
>
> *Col 3:12–17*
>
> *Rom 8:31b–35, 37, 39*
>
> *Eph 4:25–5:1–2*
>
> *1 Jn 4:7–12*
>
> *Mt 5:22–24*
>
> *Mt 5:13–16*
>
> *Jn 5:12–16*
>
> *Jn 5:9–12*

Called to Reconciliation

Gathering

Opening reflection music

> *(extended listening)*

Prayer

> *(stand)*
>
> Let us pray.
>
> Servant God,
> how often you have bowed to our needs—
> sustaining, freeing, reconciling, loving us.
>
> Because you call us to do the same for one another
> we need your healing.
>
> Help us to become true ministers,
> imitating the spirit of your son, Jesus.
>
> We ask this in his name.

All: **Amen.**

Celebration of the Word of God

First reading: *Is 42:1–4, 6–9*

> *(period of silence)*

Response

Second reading: *Acts 20:16–25, 28, 32–38*

> *(period of silence)*

Gospel acclamation

Gospel: *Jn 21:15–17*

Scripture reflection

> *(period of silence)*

Celebration of Reconciliation

(kneel)

We know our sinfulness interferes with our ability to serve the Lord and each other. Let us place this burden before God.

All:

> **I confess to you, my saving God,**
> **and to all your people,**
> **those here present,**
> **and those of all places and times,**
> **that I, like Paul and Peter,**
> **have led others away from you.**
>
> **Like them, I admit my sin.**
>
> **Be merciful to me.**
>
> **I ask the prayers of Paul and Peter,**
> **and those of all I have turned from you.**
>
> **I want to be a witness**
> **of your love and care**
> **to your people,**
> **and be ready to praise you forever.**

Song of sorrow

Prayer of reconciliation

> We know Jesus reaches out to us as he did to Peter. He wants us to return, to help establish a community of faithful love, true peace, and genuine justice.
>
> Can we answer Jesus as Peter did?
>
> *(pause)*

Leader:

Do you love me?	**Yes, Lord, you know that I love you.**
(pause)	
Will you listen to my word?	**Yes, Lord, you know that I love you.**
Will you grow into conversion?	**Yes, Lord, you know that I love you.**
Will you risk new ways of service?	**Yes, Lord, you know that I love you.**
Will you believe I make your ministry life-giving?	**Yes, Lord, you know that I love you.**
(pause)	

Will you be a sign of reconciliation?	**Yes, Lord, you know that I love you.**
Will you trust my Holy Spirit?	**Yes, Lord, you know that I love you.**
Will you discern for the good of everyone?	**Yes, Lord, you know that I love you.**

(pause)

Will you build up the community?	**Yes, Lord, you know that I love you.**
Will you support the weary?	**Yes, Lord, you know that I love you.**
Will you serve for the sake of establishing my presence?	**Yes, Lord, you know that I love you.**

(pause)

Will you bring freedom to the oppressed?	**Yes, Lord, you know that I love you.**
Will you be a light for the sightless?	**Yes, Lord, you know that I love you.**
Will you work for justice?	**Yes, Lord, you know that I love you.**

Lord's Prayer

(stand)

Let us pray together the greatest prayer of reconciliation we know. Our Father . . .

Sign of peace

Reconciliation means peace, the peace of Jesus. Let us share this peace, and be reconciled.

Conclusion

Reflection music

(continued extended listening)

Resources
Called to Reconciliation

Scripture reflection suggestions for *Is 42:1–4, 6–9; Acts 20:16–25, 28, 32–38* and *Jn 21:15–17*

Each of the readings contains major ideas for prayerful consideration by people who exercise a leadership ministry in the faith community. A reflection could center on one of these ideas:

1. God's Spirit calls leaders to act with gentleness, but with justice (*Is 42:1–4*). They are bearers of light and freedom to the community (*Is 42:6–7*), working through their own experiences of darkness and bondage. Their understanding of the law is shaped by the compassion Jesus teaches. They are asked to work for the good of all, while listening for and discerning new directions within the community (*Is 42:9*). This struggle to hear and obey the spirit in the community is the service of leadership.

   - What qualities of this leadership do I exercise?

   - How open am I to the Holy Spirit?

   - Where do I need growth as a leader?

2. In *Acts 20:16–38*, Luke presents Paul's farewell, really Paul's last will and testament, to the Ephesians. Paul tells them what dedication to the ministry of leadership means. He urges the leaders to be devoted and holy as they care for the community.

Some of the points he makes are

   - Leaders are ministers who model repentance and faith in Jesus (*Acts 20:21*). Do I trust that it is God who will accomplish the work of ministry in me, no matter what my talents, or lack thereof?

   - The Word of God builds up the community and reminds it of its identity (*Acts 20:32*). How do I allow the scripture to shape my life?

   - Leaders are ministers who serve out of the honesty and integrity of their own relationship with God. They have grown through change and conversion (*Acts 20:19–20*). How has my relationship with God grown over the years?

   - The ministry of leadership is hard work, done to help strengthen the community (*Acts 20:35*). How willing am I to work for God and not expect a tangible reward?

   - When we respond to God's call to serve in ministry, God often leads us on to other areas of ministry, calling forth more gifts from within us (*Acts 20:22–24*). How freely do I move with the Spirit's call to minister?

3. Peter's conversion from self-importance, fear, and lack of faith prepared him to serve as the leader of the church after Jesus' Ascension. As he states his love for Jesus three times, Jesus asks him to watch carefully over the community. It seems that self-importance, fear, and lack of faith are obstacles to the ministry of leadership.

- In my ministry, are my eyes on Jesus or on me?

- Do I have fears that prevent me from actively using my gifts in the service of others?

- How deeply do I believe that it is God who brings life out of the ministry I do?

Music suggestions

Opening/closing reflection music

"Jesus Your Light," (*Bless the Lord* Taizé chants with English verses, Oregon Catholic Press Publications)

"Healer of My Soul," by John Michael Talbot
(*The God of Life*, Birdwing, Sparrow Records, Inc.)

Response

"Path of Life," by Mike Balhoff, Darryl Ducote, Gary Daigle
(*Glory and Praise*)

"Service," by Buddy Ceasar (*Glory and Praise*)

"Turn To Me," by John Foley, S.J. (*Glory and Praise*)

"Yahweh, The Faithful One," by Dan Schutte (*Glory and Praise*)

"Servant Song," by Rory Cooney (*Glory and Praise*)

"Remember Your Love," by Mike Balhoff, Darryl Ducote, Gary Daigle
(*Glory and Praise*)

Gospel acclamation

"Alleluia," by Joe Wise (*Gather to Remember*)

Gospel acclamation, Nineteenth Sunday in Ordinary Time
(*Respond and Acclaim, 1995*, Oregon Catholic Press)

Song of sorrow

"We Come To Ask Forgiveness," by Carey Landry (*Glory and Praise*)

"Pardon Your People," by Carey Landry (*Glory and Praise*)

Environment suggestions

The work of reconciliation can be very difficult, especially if a person exercises the ministry of leadership. Again, we need the Scripture placed prominently but simply in our midst. Use the colors of the season to highlight the book, the stand, and the space in which the Bible is placed. Set up a container with incense near the Scripture. (A pottery or metal bowl filled with sand and a piece of charcoal works well.) The burning incense will symbolize our prayer of sorrow and our desire for reconciliation.

Further suggestions

1. The *opening reflection music* should be playing while the assembly gathers. It serves as centering prayer, so it can continue until the lay leader of prayer determines the assembly is ready to pray the beginning prayer.

2. The prayer leader can come from the assembly to lead the beginning prayer.

3. As the period of silence after the Scripture reflection concludes, add incense to the charcoal that should have been lit at the beginning of the service. The incense can burn for the rest of the service. If it grows weak, add more during the *prayer of reconciliation* because, at that point, it is well to call attention to our earnest desire for oneness with God. (The pauses provided in the prayer make it easy to do this.)

4. The *prayer of reconciliation* is best led by one person in order to make clear its nature as a dialogue.

5. The service concludes with the *opening reflection music* which recalls the penitential nature of the prayer celebrated. This atmosphere provides additional time for meditation on the Scriptures and the prayer experience shared. Ending this way allows persons to conclude when they are ready and leave individually. The music can continue as long as necessary.

Scripture Passages for
Penitential Services 1–6

At Advent Time

Cycle A **The Coming of God's Reign**
First reading: *Is 11:1–10*
Responsorial psalm: *Ps 72:1–2, 5, 10–15, 17–19*
Gospel: *Mt 11:2–11*
Proclamation of praise: *Ps 18:1–4, 17, 20, 28, 31–32, 36–37, 47*

Cycle B **Waiting in Joyful Hope**
First reading: *2 Pt 3:8–14*
Gospel: *Mk 13:33–37*

Cycle C **Bringing God to Birth**
First reading: *Is 7:14*
Second reading: *Gal 4:4–7*
Gospel: *Lk 1:39–45*

At Lenten Time

Cycle A **Walking in the Light**
First reading: *Eph 5:8–20*
Responsorial Psalm: *Ps 27:1, 7–14*
Gospel: *Mt 20:30–34*
Proclamation of praise: *Ps. 32:1–7, 10–11*

Cycle B **Keeping the Covenant**
First reading: *Jer 31:31–34*
Responsorial psalm: *Ps 111:2–10*
Gospel: *Mk 12:28–34*

Cycle C **Becoming A New Creation**
First reading: *Ez 36:24–28*
Responsorial Psalm: *Ps 51:3–21*
Second reading: *2 Cor 5:17–21*
Gospel: *Lk 22:31–34*
Proclamation of praise: *Ps 34:2, 4–9, 12–19, 22–23*

Penitential Services 7–10

At Times of Renewal, Recommitment, and New Beginnings

Living in the Spirit
Reading: *Gal 5:13–15, 18–25*
Responsorial Psalm: *Ps 130:1–8*

Being Lost, Being Found
First reading: *Jer 29:11–13*
Responsorial Psalm: *Ps 139:1–18, 23–24*
Second reading: *1 Jn 5:13–15*
Gospel: *Lk 15:1–3, 8–10*

Forgiving in Love (Communal Celebration for Couples)
Reading: *Col. 3:12–17*
Responsorial Psalm: *Ps 145:8–10, 15, 17–18*

Forgiving in Love (Celebration for Individual Couples)
Reading: personal choice or taken from resources listed

Called to Reconciliation
First reading: *Is 42:1–4, 6–9*
Second reading: *Acts 20:16–25, 28, 32–38*
Gospel: *Jn 21:15–17*

Bibliography

Confraternity of Christian Doctrine. *The Psalms, New American Bible* edition. Collegeville, Minn.: The Liturgical Press, 1991.

Donnelly, Doris. *Learning To Forgive.* Nashville, Tenn.: Abdingdon Press, 1985.

Duggan, Robert D. "Communal Penance, Three Suggestions," *Church* (Winter 1994): 39-40.

International Committee on English in the Liturgy. *Liturgical Psalter.* Chicago: Liturgy Training Publications, 1995.

Kennedy, Robert J., ed. *Reconciliation: The Continuing Agenda.* Collegeville, Minn.: The Liturgical Press, 1987.

Martos, Joseph. *Doors to the Sacred.* Garden City, N.J.: Image Books, 1982.

National Conference of Catholic Bishops. *The Rite of Penance.* New York: Catholic Book Publishing Co., 1975.

Osborn, Kenan B. *Sacramental Theology: A General Introduction.* Mahwah, N.J.: Paulist Press, 1988.

Richstatter, O.F.M. Rev. Thomas. *The Reconciliation of Penitents.* Washington, D.C.: Federation of Diocesan Liturgical Commissions, 1987.

Music Publishers and Distributors

Credence Cassettes
115 E. Armour Blvd
Kansas City, MO 64141

Steven Halpern
Daniel Kobialka
Mike Rowland

. . . .

EMI Christian Music
Nashville, TN
(615) 371-4300

Daniel Iverson

. . . .

G.I.A. Publications
7404 S. Mason Ave.
Chicago, IL 60638

Gather to Remember
composers: listed in Resources

. . . .

Music Design, Inc.
4650 N. Port Washington Rd.
Milwaukee, WI 53212
(414) 961-8380

composers: listed in Resources

. . . .

North American Liturgy Resources
(NALR)
As of 1995, NALR products and com-
posers have a new home at Oregon
Catholic Press Publications
See Address below

Glory and Praise

. . . .

Oregon Catholic Press Publications
5536 N. E. Hassalo
Portland, OR 97213
800-548-8749

Music Issue
Respond and Acclaim
composers: listed in Resources
Birdwing/Sparrow—Talbot

. . . .

World Library Publications
3759 Willow Rd.
Schiller Park, IL 60176

People's Mass Book

Acknowledgments

For permission to reprint all works in this volume, grateful acknowledgment is made to the following holders of copyright, publishers, or representatives.

Introduction

Excerpt from the *New Jerusalem Bible*, © 1985 by Darton, Longman & Todd, Ltd. and Doubleday, a division of Bantam Doubleday Dell Publishing Group, Inc. Reprinted by permission.

Service 3

Excerpt from *Litany of Mary of Nazareth*, © 1987. Used by permission of Pax Christi USA.

Service 9

Together for Life by Joseph Champlin, © 1988. Used with permission from Ave Maria Press, Notre Dame, Indiana.

Thanks to Jeanne Koma, H.M., Pastoral Counselor, for the idea of "Forgiving in Love" (celebration for individual couples).

Evaluation Form

Dear Colleagues in Ministry,

The author and publisher of *Celebrating Reconciliation* would welcome your comments after using this resource. Your observations and comments will assist us in our refinement process.

We invite you to take a few moments to fill out this simple evaluation form and return it to us with your comments.

Please do not use the original evaluation form. Make a copy for the reconciliation service(s) you want to comment on and return copy(ies) to

> The Center for Learning
> 21590 Center Ridge Road
> Rocky River, OH 44116

Name of penitential service used _____

Page number _____

1. What parts of this penitential service worked well for your assembly?

2. What elements of this penitential service were inadequate for your assembly?

3. What additions or deletions would you make to improve this penitential service?

Your Name _____

Address _____

City/State/Zip _____

The Publisher

All instructional materials identified by the TAP® (Teachers/Authors/Publishers) trademark are developed by a national network of teachers whose collective educational experience distinguishes the publishing objective of The Center for Learning, a nonprofit educational corporation founded in 1970.

Concentrating on values-related disciplines, the Center publishes humanities and religion curriculum units for use in public and private schools and other educational settings. Approximately 500 language arts, social studies, novel/drama, life issues, and faith publications are available.

While acutely aware of the challenges and uncertain solutions to growing educational problems, the Center is committed to quality curriculum development and to the expansion of learning opportunities for all students. Publications are regularly evaluated and updated to meet the changing and diverse needs of teachers and students. Teachers may offer suggestions for development of new publications or revisions of existing titles by contacting

The Center for Learning

Administrative/Editorial Office
21590 Center Ridge Rd.
Rocky River, OH 44116
(440) 331-1404 • FAX (440) 331-5414
E-mail: cfl@stratos.net
Web: http://www.centerforlearning.org

For a free catalog containing order and price information and a descriptive listing of titles, contact

The Center for Learning

Shipping/Business Office
P.O. Box 910
Villa Maria, PA 16155
(724) 964-8083 • (800) 767-9090
FAX (888) 767-8080